The Puritan by Thomas Middleton

or The Widow of Watling Street

The play was almost certainly written in 1606.

Thomas Middleton was born in London in April 1580 and baptised on 18th April.

Middleton was aged only five when his father died. His mother remarried but this unfortunately fell apart into a fifteen year legal dispute regarding the inheritance due Thomas and his younger sister.

By the time he left Oxford, at the turn of the Century, Middleton had and published Microcynicon: Six Snarling Satirese which was denounced by the Archbishop of Canterbury and publicly burned.

In the early years of the 17th century, Middleton wrote topical pamphlets. One – Penniless Parliament of Threadbare Poets was reprinted several times and the subject of a parliamentary inquiry.

These early years writing plays continued to attract controversy. His writing partnership with Thomas Dekker brought him into conflict with Ben Jonson and George Chapman in the so-called War of the Theatres.

His finest work with Dekker was undoubtedly The Roaring Girl, a biography of the notorious Mary Frith.

In the 1610s, Middleton began another playwriting partnership, this time with the actor William Rowley, producing another slew of plays including Wit at Several Weapons and A Fair Quarrel.

The ever adaptable Middleton seemed at ease working with others or by himself. His solo writing credits include the comic masterpiece, A Chaste Maid in Cheapside, in 1613.

In 1620 he was officially appointed as chronologer of the City of London, a post he held until his death.

The 1620s saw the production of his and Rowley's tragedy, and continual favourite, The Changeling, and of several other tragicomedies.

However in 1624, he reached a peak of notoriety when his dramatic allegory A Game at Chess was staged by the King's Men. Though Middleton's approach was strongly patriotic, the Privy Council silenced the play after only nine performances at the Globe theatre, having received a complaint from the Spanish ambassador.

What happened next is a mystery. It is the last play recorded as having being written by Middleton.

Thomas Middleton died at his home at Newington Butts in Southwark in the summer of 1627, and was buried on July 4th, in St Mary's churchyard which today survives as a public park in Elephant and Castle.

Index Of Contents

Dramatis Personae

Lady Plus, a citizen's WIDOW
FRANK   }
MOLL   } her two daughters
SIR GODFREY Plus, brother-in-law to the Widow Plus
Master EDMOND, son to the Widow Plus
George PYEBOARD, a scholar and a citizen
Peter SKIRMISH, an old soldier
Captain CAPTAIN IDLE, a highwayman
Corporal CORPORAL OATH, a vainglorious fellow
NICHOLAS St. Tantlings   }
SIMON St. Mary-Overies   } serving-men to the Lady Plus
FRAILTY   }
SIR OLIVER Muckhill, a rich city knight and suitor to the Lady Plus
SIR JOHN Pennydub, a country knight and suitor to Moll
SIR ANDREW Tipstaff, a courtier and suitor to Frank
The SHERIFF of London

PUTTOCK   }
RAVENSHAW   } two of the sheriff's sergeants
DOGSON, a yeoman
A NOBLEMAN
A GENTLEMAN Citizen
A KEEPER in the Marshalsea Prison
SERVANTS to the Gentleman and Sir Oliver Muckhill
Officers, Musicians, and Attendants

THE SCENE - London

ACT I

SCENE I - A Garden Behind the Widow's House

Enter the **WIDOW PLUS**, her two daughters **FRANK** and **MOLL**, her husband's brother, an old knight, **SIR GODFREY**, with her son and heir, Master **EDMOND**, all in mourning apparel, **EDMOND** in a cypress hat, the **WIDOW** wringing her hands and bursting out into passion, as newly come from the burial of her husband.

WIDOW
Oh, that ever I was born, that ever I was born!

SIR GODFREY
Nay, good sister, dear sister, sweet sister, be of good comfort; show yourself a woman now or never.

WIDOW
Oh, I have lost the dearest man, I have buried the sweetest husband that ever lay by woman!

SIR GODFREY
Nay, give him his due, he was indeed an honest, virtuous, discreet, wise man. He was my brother, as right as right.

WIDOW
Oh, I shall never forget him, never forget him! He was a man so well given to a woman. Oh!

SIR GODFREY
Nay, but, kind sister, I could weep as much as any woman; but, alas, our tears cannot call him again. Methinks you are well read, sister, and know that death is as common as homo, a common name to all men. A man shall be taken when he's making water. Nay, did not the learned parson, Master Pigman, tell us e'en now that all flesh is frail, we are born to die, man has but a time, with such-like deep and profound persuasions, as he is a rare fellow, you know, and an excellent reader. And for example, as there are examples abundance, did not Sir Humphrey Bubble die t'other day? There's a lusty widow!

Why, she cry'd not above half an hour! For shame, for shame! Then followed him old Master Fulsome, the usurer; there's a wise widow: why, she cry'd ne'er a whit at all.

WIDOW
Oh, rank not me with those wicked women; I had a husband out-shin'd 'em all!

SIR GODFREY
Ay, that he did, i'faith; he out-shin'd 'em all.

WIDOW [To **EDMOND**]
Dost thou stand there and see us all weep, and not once shed a tear for thy father's death? Oh, thou ungracious son and heir, thou!

EDMOND
Troth, mother, I should not weep, I'm sure. I am past a child, I hope, to make all my old schoolfellows laugh at me; I should be mock'd, so I should. Pray let one of my sisters weep for me. I'll laugh as much for her another time.

WIDOW
Oh, thou past-grace, thou! Out of my sight, thou graceless imp! Thou grievest me more than the death of thy father. Oh, thou stubborn only son! Hadst thou such an honest man to thy father, that would deceive all the world to get riches for thee, and canst thou not afford a little salt water? He that so wisely did quite overthrow the right heir of those lands, which now you respect not: up every morning betwixt four and five, so duly at Westminster Hall every term-time, with all his cards and writings, for thee, thou wicked Absalom! Oh, dear husband!

EDMOND
Weep, quoth 'a? I protest I am glad he's church'd, for now he's gone, I shall spend in quiet.

FRANK
Dear mother, pray cease; half your tears suffice:
'Tis time for you to take truce with your eyes;
Let me weep now.

WIDOW
Oh, such a dear knight, such a sweet husband have I lost, have I lost! If blessed be the corse the rain rains upon, he had it pouring down.

SIR GODFREY
Sister, be of good cheer; we are all mortal ourselves. I come upon you freshly. I ne'er speak without comfort. Hear me what I shall say: my brother has left you wealthy; y'are rich.

WIDOW
Oh!

SIR GODFREY
I say y'are rich. You are also fair.

WIDOW
Oh!

SIR GODFREY
Go to, y'are fair. You cannot smother it: beauty will come to light. Nor are your years so far enter'd with you but that you will be sought after, and may very well answer another husband. The world is full of fine gallants; choice enow, sister: for what should we do with all our knights, I pray, but to marry rich widows, wealthy citizens' widows, lusty, fair-brow'd ladies? Go to, be of good comfort, I say; leave snobbing and weeping. [Aside] Yet my brother was a kind-hearted man. I would not have the elf see me now.—Come, pluck up a woman's heart. Here stand your daughters, who be well estated, and at maturity will also be enquir'd after with good husbands; so all these tears shall be soon dry'd up, and a better world than ever. What, woman! You must not weep still; he's dead, he's buried. [Aside] Yet I cannot choose but weep for him.

WIDOW
Marry again! No, let me be buried quick then,
And that same part o' the choir whereon I tread
To such intent, oh, may it be my grave!
And that the priest may turn his wedding prayers,
E'en with a breath, to funeral dust and ashes!
Oh, out of a million of millions, I should ne'er find such a husband; he was unmatchable, unmatchable. Nothing was too hot nor too dear for me. I could not speak of that one thing that I had not. Beside, I had keys of all, kept all, receiv'd all, had money in my purse, spent what I would, went abroad when I would, came home when I would, and did all what I would. Oh, my sweet husband! I shall never have the like.

SIR GODFREY
Sister, ne'er say so. He was an honest brother of mine, and so; and you may light upon one as honest again, or one as honest again may light upon you: that's the properer phrase indeed.

WIDOW [Kneeling]
Never. Oh, if you love me, urge it not.
Oh, may I be the byword of the world,
The common talk at table in the mouth
Of every groom and waiter, if e'er more
I entertain the carnal suit of man.

MOLL [Kneeling]
I must kneel down for fashion too.

FRANK [Kneeling]
And I, whom never man as yet hath scal'd,
E'en in this depth of general sorrow, vow
Never to marry, to sustain such loss
As a dear husband seems to be, once dead.

MOLL
I lov'd my father well too; but to say,
Nay, vow, I would not marry for his death,

Sure I should speak false Latin, should I not?
I'd as soon vow never to come in bed.
Tut! Women must live by th' quick and not by th' dead.

WIDOW
Dear copy of my husband, oh, let me kiss thee!

[Kisses his picture.]

How like him is this model! This brief picture
Quickens my tears: my sorrows are renew'd
At this fresh sight.

SIR GODFREY
Sister—

WIDOW
Away!
All honesty with him is turn'd to clay.
Oh, my sweet husband! Oh!

FRANK
My dear father!

[Exeunt **WIDOW** and **FRANK**.

MOLL [Aside]
Here's a puling indeed! I think my mother weeps for all the women that ever buried husbands, for if from time to time all the widowers' tears in England had been bottled up, I do not think all would have fill'd a three-halfpenny bottle. Alas, a small matter bucks a handkercher, and sometimes the spital stands too nigh Saint Thomas a' Waterings. Well, I can mourn in good sober sort as well as another; but where I spend one tear for a dead father, I could give twenty kisses for a quick husband.

[Exit **MOLL**.

SIR GODFREY [Aside]
Well, go thy ways, old Sir Godfrey, and thou mayst be proud on't; thou hast a kind, loving sister-in-law. How constant, how passionate, how full of April the poor soul's eyes are! Well, I would my brother knew on't; he should then know what a kind wife he had left behind him. Truth, and 'twere not for shame that th' neighbours at the next garden should hear me, between joy and grief I should e'en cry outright!

[Exit **SIR GODFREY**.

EDMOND
So, a fair riddance! My father's laid in dust; his coffin and he is like a whole meat-pie, and the worms will cut him up shortly. Farewell, old dad, farewell! I'll be curb'd in no more. I perceive a son and heir may quickly be made a fool, and he will be one, but I'll take another order. Now she would have me weep for him, forsooth. And why? Because he cozen'd the right heir, being a fool, and bestow'd those lands on

me his eldest son; and therefore I must weep for him. Ha, ha! Why, all the world knows, as long as 'twas his pleasure to get me, 'twas his duty to get for me: I know the law in that point; no attorney can gull me. Well, my uncle is an old ass and an admirable coxcomb. I'll rule the roost myself; I'll be kept under no more; I know what I may do well enough by my father's copy: the law's in mine own hands now. Nay, now I know my strength, I'll be strong enough for my mother, I warrant you.

[Exit.

SCENE II - A Street

Enter George **PYEBOARD**, a scholar and a citizen, and unto him an old soldier, Peter **SKIRMISH**.

PYEBOARD
What's to be done now, old lad of war? Thou that were wont to be as hot as a turnspit, as nimble as a fencer, and as lousy as a school-master, now thou art put to silence like a sectary. War sits now like a justice of peace and does nothing. Where be your muskets, calivers and hot-shots? In Long Lane, at pawn, at pawn. Now keys are your only guns, key-guns, key-guns, and bawds the gunners. Who are your sentinels in peace and stand ready charg'd to give warning with hems, hums, and pocky coughs? Only your chambers are licens'd to play upon you, and drabs enow to give fire to 'em.

SKIRMISH
Well, I cannot tell, but I am sure it goes wrong with me, for since the ceasure of the wars I have spent above a hundred crowns out a' purse. I have been a soldier any time this forty years, and now I perceive an old soldier and an old courtier have both one destiny, and in the end turn both into hobnails.

PYEBOARD
Pretty mystery for a beggar, for indeed a hobnail is the true emblem of a beggar's shoe-sole.

SKIRMISH
I will not say but that war is a bloodsucker and so, but in my conscience—as there is no soldier but has a piece of one, though it be full of holes, like a shot ancient, no matter, 'twill serve to swear by—in my conscience, I think some kind of peace has more hidden oppressions and violent heady sins, though looking of a gentle nature, than a profess'd war.

PYEBOARD
Troth, and for mine own part, I am a poor gentleman and a scholar. I have been matriculated in the university, wore out six gowns there, seen some fools and some scholars, some of the city and some of the country, kept order, went bare-headed over the quadrangle, eat my commons with a good stomach, and battled with discretion; at last, having done many sleights and tricks to maintain my wit in use, as my brain would never endure me to be idle, I was expell'd the university only for stealing a cheese out of Jesus College.

SKIRMISH
Is't possible?

PYEBOARD

Oh, there was one Welshman, God forgive him, pursued it hard, and never left till I turn'd my staff toward London, where when I came, all my friends were pit-hol'd, gone to graves, as indeed there was but a few left before. Then was I turn'd to my wits to shift in the world, to tower among sons and heirs, and fools, and gulls, and ladies' eldest sons, to work upon nothing, to feed out of flint; and ever since has my belly been much beholden to my brain. But now to return to you, old Skirmish: I say as you say, and for my part wish a turbulency in the world, for I have nothing to lose but my wits, and I think they are as mad as they will be; and to strengthen your argument the more, I say an honest war is better than a bawdy peace, as touching my profession. The multiplicity of scholars, hatch'd and nourish'd in the idle claws of peace, makes 'em, like fishes, one devour another, and the community of learning has so play'd upon affections, and thereby almost religion is come about to fantasy, and discredited by being too much spoken of, in so many and mean mouths. I myself being a scholar and a graduate have no other comfort by my learning but the affection of my words, to know how, scholar-like, to name what I want, and can call myself a beggar both in Greek and Latin. And therefore not to cog with peace, I'll not be afraid to say 'tis a great breeder but a barren nourisher, a great getter of children which must either be thieves or rich men, knaves or beggars.

SKIRMISH
Well, would I had been born a knave then, when I was born a beggar! For if the truth were known, I think I was begot when my father had never a penny in his purse.

PYEBOARD
Puh! Faint not, old Skirmish; let this warrant thee: facilis descensus Averni; 'tis an easy journey to a knave. Thou mayst be a knave when thou wilt, and peace is good madam to all other professions, and an arrant drab to us. Let us handle her accordingly, and by our wits thrive in despite of her, for since the law lives by quarrels, the courtier by smooth good-morrows, and every profession makes itself great by imperfections, why not we then by shifts, wiles, and forgeries? And seeing our brains are our only patrimonies, let's spend with judgment, not like a desperate son and heir, but like a sober and discreet Templar, one that will never march beyond the bounds of his allowance. And for our thriving means, thus: I myself will put on the deceit of a fortune-teller.

SKIRMISH
A fortune-teller? Very proper.

PYEBOARD
And you a figure-caster or a conjurer.

SKIRMISH
A conjurer?

PYEBOARD
Let me alone; I'll instruct you and teach you to deceive all eyes but the devil's.

SKIRMISH
Oh, ay, for I would not deceive him, and I could choose, of all others.

PYEBOARD
Fear not, I warrant you. And so by those means we shall help one another to patients, as the condition of the age affords creatures enow for cunning to work upon.

SKIRMISH

Oh, wondrous! New fools and fresh asses!

PYEBOARD

Oh, fit, fit; excellent!

SKIRMISH

What, in the name of conjuring?

PYEBOARD

My memory greets me happily with an admirable subject to graze upon: the lady widow, who of late I saw weeping in her garden for the death of her husband. Sure she 'as but a waterish soul, and half of't by this time is dropp'd out of her eyes: device well manag'd may do good upon her. It stands firm; my first practice shall be there.

SKIRMISH

You have my voice, George.

PYEBOARD

Sh'as a grey gull to her brother, a fool to her only son, and an ape to her youngest daughter. I overhead 'em severally, and from their words I'll derive my device; and thou, old Peter Skirmish, shalt be my second in all sleights.

SKIRMISH

Ne'er doubt me, George Pyeboard. Only you must teach me to conjure.

PYEBOARD

Puh! I'll perfect thee, Peter.

[Enter **CAPTAIN CAPTAIN IDLE** pinioned, and with a guard of **OFFICERS** passeth over the stage.

How now! What's he?

SKIRMISH

Oh, George, this sight kills me! 'Tis my sworn brother, Captain Idle!

PYEBOARD

Captain Idle!

SKIRMISH

Apprehended for some felonious act or another. He has started out; h'as made a night on't, lack'd silver. I cannot but commend his resolution; he would not pawn his buff-jerkin. I would either some of us were employed or might pitch our tents at usurers' doors to kill the slaves as they peep out at the wicket.

PYEBOARD

Indeed, those are our ancient enemies; they keep our money in their hands, and make us to be hang'd for robbing of 'em. But come, let's follow after to the prison, and know the nature of his offence; and what we can stead him in, he shall be sure of. And I'll uphold it still, that a charitable knave is better than a soothing Puritan.

[Exeunt.

SCENE III - A Street

Enter at one door **CORPORAL CORPORAL OATH**, a vainglorious fellow, and at the other, three of the Widow Puritan's serving-men; **NICHOLAS** St. Tantlings, **SIMON** St. Mary-Overies, and **FRAILITY**, in black scurvy mourning coats, and books at their girdles, as coming from church. They meet.

NICHOLAS
What, Corporal Oath! I am sorry we have met with you, next our hearts; you are the man that we are forbidden to keep company withal. We must not swear, I can tell you, and you have the name for swearing.

SIMON
Ay, Corporal Oath, I would you would do so much as forsake us, sir. We cannot abide you; we must not be seen in your company.

FRAILTY
There is none of us, I can tell you, but shall be soundly whipp'd for swearing.

CORPORAL OATH
Why, how now, we three? Puritanical scrape-shoes, flesh o' Good Fridays, a hand!

[Shakes them by the hand.

ALL [THREE SERVING-MEN]
Oh!

CORPORAL OATH
Why, Nicholas St. Tantlings, Simon St. Mary-Overies, has the de'il possess'd you that you swear no better? You half-christen'd catamites, you ungodmother'd varlets! Does the first lesson teach you to be proud, and the second to be coxcombs? Proud coxcombs, not once to do duty to a man of mark!

FRAILTY
A man of mark, quoth 'a? I do not think he can show a beggar's noble.

CORPORAL OATH
A corporal, a commander, one of spirit, that is able to blow you up all three with your books at your girdles.

NICHOLAS
We are not taught to believe that, sir, for we know the breath of man is weak.

[**CORPORAL OATH** breathes upon **FRAILITY**.

FRAILTY
Foh! You lie, Nicholas, for here's one strong enough! Blow us up, quoth 'a? He may well blow me above twelve-score off a' him: I warrant, if the wind stood right, a man might smell him from the top of Newgate to the leads of Ludgate.

CORPORAL OATH
Sirrah, thou hollow book of wax-candle—

NICHOLAS
Ay, you may say what you will, so you swear not.

CORPORAL OATH
I swear by the—

NICHOLAS
Hold, hold, good Corporal Oath, for if you swear once, we shall all fall down in a swoon presently!

CORPORAL OATH
I must and will swear, you quivering coxcombs. My captain is imprison'd, and by Vulcan's leather cod-piece point—

NICHOLAS
Oh, Simon, what an oath was there!

FRAILTY
If he should chance to break it, the poor man's breeches would fall down about his heels, for Venus allows him but one point to his hose.

CORPORAL OATH
With these my bully feet I will thump ope the prison doors, and brain the keeper with the begging-box, but I'll see my honest, sweet Captain Idle at liberty.

NICHOLAS
How, Captain Idle? My old aunt's son, my dear kinsman, in cappadochio?

CORPORAL OATH
Ay, thou church pealing, thou holy paring, religious outside, thou! If thou hadst any grace in thee, thou wouldst visit him, relieve him, swear to get him out.

NICHOLAS
Assure you, corporal, indeed, la, 'tis the first time I heard on't.

CORPORAL OATH
Why, do't now then, marmoset! Bring forth thy yearly wages; let not a commander perish.

SIMON

But if he be one of the wicked, he shall perish.

NICHOLAS
Well, corporal, I'll e'en along with you to visit my kinsman; if I can do him any good, I will, but I have nothing for him. Simon St. Mary-Overies and Frailty, pray make a lie for me to the knight my master, old Sir Godfrey.

CORPORAL OATH
A lie! May you lie then?

FRAILTY
Oh, ay, we may lie, but must not swear.

SIMON
True, we may lie with our neighbour's wife, but we must not swear we did so.

CORPORAL OATH
Oh, an excellent tag of religion!

NICHOLAS
Oh, Simon, I have thought upon a sound excuse; it will go current: say that I am gone to a fast.

SIMON
To a fast? Very good.

NICHOLAS
Ay, to a fast, say, with Master Fullbelly the minister.

SIMON
Master Fullbelly? An honest man; he feeds the flock well, for he's an excellent feeder.

[Exit **CORPORAL OATH** with **NICHOLAS**.

FRAILTY
Oh, ay, I have seen him eat up a whole pig, and afterward fall to the pettitoes.

[Exeunt **SIMON** and **FRAILITY**.

SCENE V - Captain Idle's Cell in the Marshalsea Prison

Enter **CAPTAIN CAPTAIN IDLE** at one door, and later **PYEBOARD** and the old soldier **SKIRMISH** at the other.

PYEBOARD [speaking within]
Pray turn the key.

SKIRMISH [Within]
Turn the key, I pray.

CAPTAIN IDLE
Who should those be? I almost know their voices.

[**PYEBOARD** and **SKIRMISH** entering.

Oh, my friends!
You are welcome to a smelling room here.
You new took leave of the air; has it not a strange savour?

PYEBOARD
As all prisons have, smells of sundry wretches
Who, though departed, leave their scents behind 'em.
By gold, captain, I am sincerely sorry for thee.

CAPTAIN IDLE
By my troth, George, I thank thee. But pish, what must be, must be.

SKIRMISH
Captain, what do you lie in for? Is't great? What's your offence?

CAPTAIN IDLE
Faith, my offence is ordinary, common: a highway; and I fear me my penalty will be ordinary and common too: a halter.

PYEBOARD
Nay, prophesy not so ill; it shall go hard but I'll shift for thy life.

CAPTAIN IDLE
Whether I live or die, thou art an honest George. I'll tell you: silver flow'd not with me as it had done, for now the tide runs to bawds and flatterers. I had a start out, and by chance set upon a fat steward, thinking his purse had been as pursy as his body, and the slave had about him but the poor purchase of ten groats; notwithstanding, being descried, pursued, and taken, I know the law is so grim, in respect of many desperate, unsettled soldiers, that I fear me I shall dance after their pipe for't.

SKIRMISH
I am twice sorry for you, captain: first, that your purchase was so small, and now that your danger is so great.

CAPTAIN IDLE
Push! The worst is but death. Ha' you a pipe of tobacco about you?

SKIRMISH
I think I have thereabouts about me.

CAPTAIN IDLE

Here's a clean gentleman too to receive.

[**CAPTAIN IDLE** blows a pipe.

PYEBOARD
Well, I must cast about some happy sleight.
Work brain, that ever didst thy master right!

CORPORAL OATH [within]
Keeper, let the key be turn'd!

NICHOLAS within
Ay, I pray, master keeper, give 's a cast of your office.

[Enter **CORPORAL OATH** and **NICHOLAS**.

CAPTAIN IDLE
How now? More visitants? What, Corporal Oath?

PYEBOARD, SKIRMISH
Corporal.

CORPORAL OATH
In prison, honest captain? This must not be.

NICHOLAS
How do you, captain kinsman?

CAPTAIN IDLE [To **CORPORAL OATH**]
Good coxcomb! What makes that pure, starch'd fool here?

NICHOLAS
You see, kinsman, I am somewhat bold to call in and see how you do. I heard you were safe enough, and I was very glad on't that it was no worse.

CAPTAIN IDLE
This is a double torture now. This fool, by th' book,
Does vex me more than my imprisonment.
What meant you, corporal, to hook him hither?

CORPORAL OATH
Who, he? He shall relieve thee and supply thee; I'll make him do't.

CAPTAIN IDLE [Taking **CORPORAL OATH** aside]
Fie, what vain breath you spend! He supply? I'll sooner expect mercy from a usurer when my bond's forfeited, sooner kindness from a lawyer when my money's spent, nay, sooner charity from the devil than good from a Puritan. I'll look for relief from him when Lucifer is restor'd to his blood and in heaven again!

NICHOLAS
I warrant my kinsman's talking of me, for my left ear burns tyrannically.

[**PYEBOARD** and **SKIRMISH** join **CAPTAIN IDLE** and **CORPORAL OATH**.

PYEBOARD
Captain Idle, what's he there? He looks like a monkey upward and a crane downward.

CAPTAIN IDLE
Pshaw! A foolish cousin of mine; I must thank God for him.

PYEBOARD
Why, the better subject to work a 'scape upon; thou shalt e'en change clothes with him and leave him here, and so—

CAPTAIN IDLE
Push! I publish'd him e'en now to my corporal: he will be damn'd ere he do me so much good. Why, I know a more proper, a more handsome device than that, if the slave would be sociable.—Now, goodman Fleerface?

NICHOLAS [Aside]
Oh, my cousin begins to speak to me now; I shall be acquainted with him again, I hope.

SKIRMISH
Look what ridiculous raptures take hold of his wrinkles!

PYEBOARD
Then what say you to this device? A happy one, captain?

CAPTAIN IDLE
Speak low, George; prison-rats have wider ears than those in malt-lofts.

[**PYEBOARD** whispers to them.

NICHOLAS
Cousin, if it lay in my power, as they say—to—do—

CAPTAIN IDLE
'Twould do me an exceeding pleasure indeed, that; but ne'er talk further on't: the fool will be hang'd ere he do't.

CORPORAL OATH
Pox, I'll thump 'im to't!

PYEBOARD
Why, do but try the fopster, and break it to him bluntly.

CAPTAIN IDLE

And so my disgrace will dwell in his jaws, and the slave slaver out our purpose to his master, for would I were but as sure on't as I am sure he will deny to do't.

NICHOLAS

I would be heartily glad, cousin, if any of my friendships, as they say, might—stand—ah—

PYEBOARD

Why, you see he offers his friendship foolishly to you already.

CAPTAIN IDLE

Ay, that's the hell on't; I would he would offer it wisely.

NICHOLAS

Verily and indeed, la, cousin—

CAPTAIN IDLE [To **NICHOLAS**]

I have took note of thy fleers a good while. If thou art minded to do me good—as thou gap'st upon me comfortably and giv'st me charitable faces, which indeed is but a fashion in you all that are Puritans— wilt soon at night steal me thy master's chain?

NICHOLAS

Oh, I shall swoon!

PYEBOARD

Corporal, he starts already.

CAPTAIN IDLE

I know it to be worth three hundred crowns, and with half of that I can buy my life at a broker's at second-hand, which now lies in pawn to the law. If this thou refuse to do, being easy and nothing dangerous, in that thou art held in good opinion of thy master, why 'tis a palpable argument thou hold'st my life at no price, and these thy broken and unjointed offers are but only created in thy lip, now born and now buried, foolish breath only. What, woult do't? Shall I look for happiness in thy answer?

NICHOLAS

Steal my master's chain, quoth 'a? No, it shall ne'er be said that Nicholas St. Tantlings committed bird-lime.

CAPTAIN IDLE [To **PYEBOARD**]

Nay, I told you as much, did I not? Though he be a Puritan, yet he will be a true man.

NICHOLAS

Why, cousin, you know 'tis written, "Thou shalt not steal."

CAPTAIN IDLE

Why, and fool, "Thou shalt love thy neighbour," and help him in extremities.

NICHOLAS

Mass, I think it be indeed: in what chapter's that, cousin?

CAPTAIN IDLE
Why, in the first of Charity, the second verse.

NICHOLAS
The first of Charity, quoth 'a? That's a good jest; there's no such chapter in my book.

CAPTAIN IDLE
No, I knew 'twas torn out of thy book, and that makes it so little in thy heart.

PYEBOARD [Taking **NICHOLAS** aside]
Come, let me tell you, y'are too unkind a kinsman, i'faith, the captain loving you so dearly, ay, like the pomewater of his eye, and you to be so uncomfortable: fie, fie!

NICHOLAS
Pray do not wish me to be hang'd. Anything else that I can do, had it been to rob, I would ha' done't, but I must not steal: that's the word, the literal "Thou shalt not steal;" and would you wish me to steal then?

PYEBOARD
No, faith, that were too much, to speak truth. Why, woult thou nim it from him?

NICHOLAS
That I will.

PYEBOARD
Why, enough, bully; he shall be content with that or he shall ha' none. Let me alone with him now.— Captain, I ha' dealt with your kinsman in a corner; a good, kind-natur'd fellow, methinks. Go to, you shall not have all your own asking; you shall bate somewhat on't: he is not contented absolutely, as you would say, to steal the chain from him, but to do you a pleasure, he will nim it from him.

NICHOLAS
Ay, that I will, cousin.

CAPTAIN IDLE
Well, seeing he will do no more, as far as I see, I must be contented with that.

CORPORAL OATH [Aside]
Here's no notable gullery!

PYEBOARD
Nay, I'll come nearer to you, gentleman. Because we'll have only but a help and a mirth on't, the knight shall not lose his chain neither, but be only laid out of the way some one or two days.

NICHOLAS
Ay, that would be good indeed, kinsman.

PYEBOARD

For I have a farther reach to profit us better by the missing on't only than if we had it outright, as my discourse shall make it known to you. When thou hast the chain, do but convey it out at back door into the garden, and there hang it close in the rosemary bank, but for a small season; and by that harmless device I know how to wind Captain Idle out of prison. The knight thy master shall get his pardon and release him, and he satisfy thy master with his own chain, and wondrous thanks on both hands.

NICHOLAS
That were rare indeed, la! Pray let me know how.

PYEBOARD
Nay, 'tis very necessary thou should'st know, because thou must be employ'd as an actor.

NICHOLAS
An actor? Oh, no, that's a player, and our parson rails again' the players mightily, I can tell you, because they brought him drunk upo' th' stage once, as he will be horribly drunk.

CORPORAL OATH
Mass, I cannot blame him then, poor church-spout.

PYEBOARD
Why, as an intermeddler then.

NICHOLAS
Ay, that, that.

PYEBOARD
Give me audience then. When the old knight thy master has rag'd his fill for the loss of the chain, tell him thou hast a kinsman in prison of such exquisite art that the devil himself is French lackey to him and runs bare-headed by his horse-belly, when he has one, whom he will cause with most Irish dexterity to fetch his chain, though 'twere hid under a mine of sea-coal and ne'er make spade or pick-axe his instruments. Tell him but this, with farther instructions thou shalt receive from me, and thou showest thyself a kinsman indeed.

CORPORAL OATH
A dainty bully.

SKIRMISH
An honest bookkeeper.

CAPTAIN IDLE
And my three times thrice honey cousin.

NICHOLAS
Nay, grace of God, I'll rob him on't suddenly, and hang it in the rosemary bank; but I bear that mind, cousin, I would not steal anything, methinks, for mine own father.

SKIRMISH
He bears a good mind in that, captain.

PYEBOARD
Why, well said; he begins to be an honest fellow, faith.

CORPORAL OATH
In troth, he does.

NICHOLAS
You see, cousin, I am willing to do you any kindness, always saving myself harmless.

CAPTAIN IDLE
Why, I thank thee. Fare thee well; I shall requite thee.

[Exit **NICHOLAS**.

CORPORAL OATH
'Twill be good for thee, captain, that thou hast such an egregious ass to thy cousin.

CAPTAIN IDLE
Ay, is he not a fine fool, corporal?
But, George, thou talk'st of art and conjuring:
How shall that be?

PYEBOARD
Puh! Be't not in your care;
Leave that to me and my directions.
Well, captain, doubt not thy delivery now,
E'en with the vantage, man, to gain by prison,
As my thoughts prompt me. Hold on, brain and plot!
I aim at many cunning far events,
All which I doubt not but to hit at length.
I'll to the widow with a quaint assault.
Captain, be merry.

CAPTAIN IDLE
Who, I? Kerry-merry-buff-jerkin!

PYEBOARD
Oh, I am happy in more sleights, and one will knit strong in another. Corporal Oath?

CORPORAL OATH
Ho, bully?

PYEBOARD
And thou, old Peter Skirmish, I have a necessary talk for you both.

SKIRMISH
Lay't upon us, George Pyeboard.

CORPORAL OATH
Whate'er it be, we'll manage it.

PYEBOARD
I would have you two maintain a quarrel before the lady widow's door, and draw your swords i' th' edge of the evening: clash a little, clash, clash.

CORPORAL OATH
Fuh! Let us alone to make our blades ring noon, though it be after supper.

PYEBOARD
I know you can, and out of that false fire, I doubt not but to raise strange belief. And, captain, to countenance my device the better, and grace my words to the widow, I have a good plain satin suit that I had of a young reveller t'other night; for words pass not regarded nowadays unless they come from a good suit of clothes, which the Fates and my wits have bestowed upon me. Well, Captain Idle, if I did not highly love thee, I would ne'er be seen within twelve score of a prison, for I protest, at this instant I walk in great danger of small debts. I owe money to several hostesses, and you know such jills will quickly be upon a man's jack.

CAPTAIN IDLE
True, George.

PYEBOARD
Fare thee well, captain. Come, corporal and ancient. Thou shalt hear more news next time we greet thee.

CORPORAL OATH
More news? Ay, by yon Bear at Bridgefoot in heaven, shalt thou!

[Exeunt **PYEBOARD, SKIRMISH**, and **CORPORAL OATH**.

CAPTAIN IDLE
Enough; my friends, farewell!
This prison shows as ghosts did part in hell.

[Exit.

ACT II

SCENE I - A Room in the Widow's House

Enter **MOLL**, youngest daughter to the Widow, alone.

MOLL

Not marry? Forswear marriage? Why, all women know 'tis as honourable a thing as to lie with a man, and I, to spite my sister's vow the more, have entertained a suitor already, a fine gallant knight of the last feather. He says he will coach me too, and well appoint me, allow me money to dice withal, and many such pleasing protestations he sticks upon my lips. Indeed, his short-winded father i' th' country is wondrous wealthy, a most abominable farmer, and therefore he may in time. Troth, I'll venture upon him. Women are not without ways enow to help themselves: if he prove wise and good as his word, why, I shall love him and use him kindly; and if he prove an ass, why, in a quarter of an hour's warning I can transform him into an ox: there comes in my relief again.

[Enter **FRAILITY**.

FRAILTY
Oh, Mistress Moll, Mistress Moll!

MOLL
How now? What's the news?

FRAILTY
The knight your suitor, Sir John Pennydub!

MOLL
Sir John Pennydub? Where, where?

FRAILTY
He's walking in the gallery.

MOLL
Has my mother seen him yet?

FRAILTY
Oh, no; she's spitting in the kitchen.

MOLL
Direct him hither softly, good Frailty; I'll meet him halfway.

FRAILTY
That's just like running a tilt, but I hope he'll break nothing this time.

[Exit.

MOLL
'Tis happiness my mother saw him not.

[Enter **SIR JOHN PENNYDUB**.

Oh, welcome, good Sir John.

SIR JOHN PENNYDUB

I thank you, faith.

[He tries to kiss her, but she rebuffs him.]

Nay, you must stand me till I kiss you: 'tis the fashion everywhere, i'faith, and I came from court e' now.

MOLL
Nay, the Fates forfend that I should anger the fashion!

SIR JOHN PENNYDUB
Then, not forgetting the sweet of new ceremonies, I first fall back; then recovering myself, make my honour to your lips thus, and then accost it.

[Kisses her.

MOLL
Trust me, very pretty and moving; y'are worthy on't, sir.

[Kissing. Enter **WIDOW** and **SIR GODFREY**.

Oh, my mother, my mother! Now she's here, we'll steal into the gallery.

[Exeunt **SIR JOHN PENNYDUB** and **MOLL**.

SIR GODFREY
Nay, sister, let reason rule you: do not play the fool; stand not in your own light. You have wealthy offers, large tend'rings; do not withstand your good fortune. Who comes a-wooing to you, I pray? No small fool; a rich knight a' th' city, Sir Oliver Muckhill: no small fool, I can tell you. And furthermore, as I heard late by your maid-servants—as your maid-servants will say to me anything, I thank 'em—both your daughters are not without suitors; ay, and worthy ones too: one a brisk courtier, Sir Andrew Tipstaff, suitor afar off to your eldest daughter, and the third a huge, wealthy farmer's son, a fine young country knight. They call him Sir John Pennydub, a good name, marry: he may have it coin'd when he lacks money. What blessings are these, sister!

WIDOW
Tempt me not, Satan.

SIR GODFREY
Satan! Do I look like Satan? I hope the devil's not so old as I, I trow.

WIDOW
You wound my senses, brother, when you name
A suitor to me. Oh, I cannot abide it!
I take in poison when I hear one nam'd.

[Enter **SIMON**.

How now, Simon? Where's my son Edmond?

SIMON
Verily, madam, he is at vain exercise, dripping in the tennis court.

WIDOW
At tennis court? Oh, now his father's gone, I shall have no rule with him! Oh, wicked Edmond! I might well compare this with the prophecy in the Chronicle, though far inferior: as Harry of Monmouth won all, and Harry of Windsor lost all, so Edmond of Bristow, that was the father, got all, and Edmond of London, that's his son, now will spend all.

SIR GODFREY
Peace, sister, we'll have him reform'd; there's hope on him yet, though it be but a little.

[Enter **FRAILITY**.

FRAILTY
Forsooth, madam, there are two or three archers at door would very gladly speak with your ladyship.

WIDOW
Archers?

SIR GODFREY
Your husband's fletcher, I warrant.

WIDOW
Oh,
Let them come near; they bring home things of his.
Troth, I should ha' forgot 'em. How now, villain!
Which be those archers?

[Enter the suitors **SIR ANDREW TIPSTAFF, SIR OLIVER MUCKHILL**, and **SIR JOHN PENNYDUB**.

FRAILTY
Why, do you not see 'em before you? Are not these archers? What do you call 'em? Shooters. Shooters and archers are all one, I hope.

WIDOW
Out, ignorant slave!

SIR OLIVER
Nay, pray be patient, lady.
We come in way of honourable love—

SIR ANDREW, SIR JOHN
We do.

SIR OLIVER
To you.

SIR ANDREW, SIR JOHN
And to your daughters.

WIDOW
Oh,
Why will you offer me this, gentlemen—
Indeed I will not look upon you—when the tears are scarce out of mine eyes, not yet wash'd off from my cheeks, and my dear husband's body scarce so cold as the coffin? What reason have you to offer it? I am not like some of your widows that will bury one in the evening and be sure to another ere morning. Pray, away; pray take your answers, good knights, and you be sweet knights. I have vow'd never to marry, and so have my daughters too.

SIR JOHN PENNYDUB [Aside]
Ay, two of you have, but the third's a good wench.

SIR OLIVER
Lady, a shrewd answer, marry. The best is, 'tis but the first, and he's a blunt wooer that will leave for one sharp answer.

SIR ANDREW
Where be your daughters, lady? I hope they'll give us better encouragements.

WIDOW
Indeed, they'll answer you so; take 't a' my word, they'll give you the very same answer verbatim, truly, la.

SIR JOHN PENNYDUB [Aside]
Mum. Moll's a good wench still; I know what she'll do.

SIR OLIVER
Well, lady, for this time we'll take our leaves, hoping for better comfort.

WIDOW
Oh, never, never, and I live these thousand years. And you be good knights, do not hope; 'twill be all vain, vain. Look you put off all your suits and you come to me again.

[Exeunt **SIR JOHN PENNYDUB** and **SIR ANDREW**.

FRAILTY [Aside]
Put off all their suits, quoth 'a? Ay, that's the best wooing of a widow indeed, when a man's non-suited, that is, when he's a-bed with her.

[Going out, **SIR OLIVER** and **SIR GODFREY**.

SIR OLIVER [Giving him money]
Sir Godfrey, here's twenty angels more. Work hard for me; there's life in't yet.

SIR GODFREY
Fear not, Sir Oliver Muckhill, I'll stick close for you; leave all with me.

[Exit **SIR OLIVER**. Enter George **PYEBOARD** the scholar.

PYEBOARD
By your leave, lady widow.

WIDOW
What, another suitor now?

PYEBOARD
A suitor! No, I protest, lady, if you'd give me yourself, I'd not be troubled with you.

WIDOW
Say you so, sir? Then you're the better welcome, sir.

PYEBOARD
Nay, heaven bless me from a widow, unless I were sure to bury her speedily!

WIDOW
Good bluntness. Well, your business, sir?

PYEBOARD
Very needful, if you were in private once.

WIDOW
Needful? Brother, pray leave us, and you, sir.

[Exit **SIR GODFREY**.

FRAILTY [Aside]
I should laugh now if this blunt fellow should put 'em all beside the stirrup and vault into the saddle himself. I have seen as mad a trick.

[Exit **FRAILITY**.

WIDOW
Now, sir, here's none but we.

[Enter daughters **MOLL** and **FRANK**.

Daughters, forbear.

PYEBOARD
Oh, no, pray let 'em stay, for what I have to speak importeth equally to them as to you.

WIDOW

Then you may stay.

PYEBOARD
I pray bestow on me a serious ear,
For what I speak is full of weight and fear.

WIDOW
Fear?

PYEBOARD
Ay, if't pass unregarded and unaffected; else peace and joy: I pray attention. Widow, I have been a mere stranger for these parts that you live in, nor did I ever know the husband of you and father of them, but I truly know by certain spiritual intelligence that he is in purgatory.

WIDOW
Purgatory! Tuh, that word deserves to be spit upon! I wonder that a man of sober tongue, as you seem to be, should have the folly to believe there's such a place.

PYEBOARD
Well, lady, in cold blood I speak it. I assure you that there is a purgatory, in which place I know your husband to reside, and wherein he is like to remain till the dissolution of the world, till the last general bonfire, when all the earth shall melt into nothing, and the seas scald their finny labourers; so long is his abidance unless you alter the property of your purpose together with each of your daughters theirs: that is, the purpose of single life in yourself and your eldest daughter, and the speedy determination of marriage in your youngest.

MOLL [Aside]
How knows he that? What, has some devil told him?

WIDOW
Strange he should know our thoughts. Why, but, daughter, have you purpos'd speedy marriage?

PYEBOARD
You see she tells you ay, for she says nothing. Nay, give me credit as your please; I am a stranger to you, and yet you see I know your determinations, which must come to me metaphysically and by a supernatural intelligence.

WIDOW
This puts amazement on me.

FRANK
Know our secrets?

MOLL [Aside]
I'd thought to steal a marriage. Would his tongue
Had dropp'd out when he blabb'd it!

WIDOW

But, sir, my husband was too honest a dealing man to be now in any purgatories.

PYEBOARD
Oh, do not load your conscience with untruths;
'Tis but mere folly now to gild him o'er
That has past but for copper. Praises here
Cannot unbind him there. Confess but truth:
I know he got his wealth with a hard gripe,
Oh, hardly, hardly!

WIDOW [Aside]
This is most strange of all: how knows her that?

PYEBOARD
He would eat fools and ignorant heirs clean up,
And had his drink from many a poor man's brow,
E'en as their labour brew'd it. He would scrape
Riches to him most unjustly: the very dirt
Between his nails was ill got and not his own.
Oh, I groan to speak on't; the thought makes me shudder,
Shudder!

WIDOW [Aside]
It quakes me too now I think on't.—
Sir, I am much griev'd that you, a stranger, should
So deeply wrong my dead husband—

PYEBOARD
Oh!

WIDOW
A man that would keep church so duly: rise early, before his servants, and e'en for religious haste, go ungarter'd, unbutton'd, nay, sir-reverence, untruss'd to morning prayer—

PYEBOARD
Oh, uff!

WIDOW
Dine quickly upon high days, and when I had great guests, would e'en shame me and rise from the table to get a good seat at an afternoon sermon.

PYEBOARD
There's the devil, there's the devil! True, he thought it sanctity enough if he had kill'd a man, so 't 'ad been done in a pew, or undone his neighbour, so 't 'ad been near enough to th' preacher. Oh, a sermon's fine short cloak of an hour long and will hide the upper part of a dissembler! Church! Ay, he seem'd all church, and his conscience was as hard as the pulpit.

WIDOW

I can no more endure this.

PYEBOARD
Nor I, widow, endure to flatter.

WIDOW
Is this all your business with me?

PYEBOARD
No, lady, 'tis but the induction to it.
You may believe my strains; I strike all true:
And if your conscience would leap up to your tongue,
Yourself would affirm it. And that you shall perceive
I know of things to come, as well as I do
Of what is present, a brother of your husband's
Shall shortly have a loss.

WIDOW
A loss? Marry, heaven forfend! Sir Godfrey, my brother?

PYEBOARD
Nay, keep in your wonders till I have told you the fortunes of you all, which are more fearful if not happily prevented. For your part and your daughters', if there be not once this day some bloodshed before your door, whereof the human creature dies, two of you, the elder, shall run mad—

WIDOW, FRANK
Oh!

MOLL
That's not I yet.

PYEBOARD
And, with most impudent prostitution, show your naked bodies to the view of all beholders.

WIDOW
Our naked bodies? Fie, for shame!

PYEBOARD
Attend me: and your younger daughter be strucken dumb.

MOLL
Dumb? Out, alas! 'Tis the worst pain of all for a woman. I'd rather be mad, or run naked, or anything. Dumb!

PYEBOARD
Give ear: ere the evening fall upon hill, bog, and meadow, this my speech shall have past probation, and then shall I be believed accordingly.

WIDOW
If this be true, we are all sham'd, all undone!

MOLL
Dumb! I'll speak as much as ever I can before evening.

PYEBOARD
But if it so come to pass, as for your fair sakes I wish it may, that this presage of your strange fortunes be prevented by that accident of death and blood-shedding, which I before told you of, take heed, upon your lives, that two of you, which have vow'd never to marry, seek out husbands with all present speed, and you, the third, that have such a desire to outstrip chastity, look you meddle not with a husband.

MOLL
A double torment!

PYEBOARD
The breach of this keep your father in purgatory, and the punishments that shall follow you in this world would with horror kill the ear should hear 'em related.

WIDOW
Marry! Why, I vow'd never to marry!

FRANK
And so did I.

MOLL [Aside]
And I vow'd never to be such an ass, but to marry. What a cross fortune's this!

PYEBOARD
Ladies, though I be a fortune-teller, I cannot better fortunes; you have 'em from me as they are reveal'd to me. I would they were to your tempers, and fellows with your bloods; that's all the bitterness I would you.

WIDOW
Oh, 'tis a just vengeance for my husband's hard purchases!

PYEBOARD
I wish you to bethink yourselves and leave 'em.

WIDOW
I'll to Sir Godfrey, my brother, and acquaint him with these fearful presages.

FRANK
For, mother, they portend losses to him.

WIDOW
Oh, ay, they do, they do.
If any happy issue crown thy words,

I will reward thy cunning.

PYEBOARD
'Tis enough, lady; I wish no higher.

[Exit **WIDOW** with **FRANK**.

MOLL
Dumb? And not marry? Worse!
Neither to speak nor kiss, a double curse.

[Exit.

PYEBOARD
So, all this comes well about yet. I play the fortune-teller as well as if I had had a witch to my grannam: for by good happiness, being in my hostess's garden, which neighbours the orchard of the widow, I laid the hole of mine ear to a hole in the wall, and heard 'em make these vows and speak those words, upon which I wrought these advantages; and to encourage my forgery the more, I may now perceive in 'em a natural simplicity which will easily swallow an abuse, if any covering be over it. And to confirm my former presage to the widow, I have advis'd old Peter Skirmish the soldier to hurt Corporal Oath upon the leg, and in that hurry I'll rush amongst 'em, and instead of giving the corporal some cordial to comfort him, I'll pour into his mouth a potion of a sleepy nature to make him seem as dead; for the which the old soldier being apprehended and ready to be borne to execution, I'll step in and take upon me the cure of the dead man upon pain of dying the condemned's death. The corporal will wake at his minute, when the sleepy force hath wrought itself, and so shall I get myself into a most admir'd opinion, and, under the pretext of that cunning, beguile as I see occasion. And if that foolish Nicholas St. Tantlings keep true time with the chain, my plot will be sound, the captain delivered, and my wits applauded among scholars and soldiers forever.

[Exit **PYEBOARD**.

SCENE II - A Garden

Enter **NICHOLAS** St. Tantlings with the chain.

NICHOLAS
Oh, I have found an excellent advantage to take away the chain! My master put it off e'en now to say on a new doublet, and I sneak'd it away by little and little, most puritanically. We shall have good sport anon, when h'as miss'd it, about my cousin the conjurer. The world shall see I'm an honest man of my word, for now I'm going to hang it between heaven and earth, among the rosemary branches.

[Exit **NICHOLAS**.

ACT III

Enter **SIMON** and **FRAILITY**.

FRAILTY
Sirrah Simon St. Mary-Overies, my mistress sends away all her suitors and puts fleas in their ears.

SIMON
Frailty, she does like an honest, chaste, and virtuous woman, for widows ought not to wallow in the puddle of iniquity.

FRAILTY
Yet, Simon, many widows will do't, whatso comes on't.

SIMON
True, Frailty, their filthy flesh desires a conjunction copulative. What strangers are within, Frailty?

FRAILTY
There's none, Simon, but Master Pilfer the tailor; he's above with Sir Godfrey, 'praising of a doublet. And I must trudge anon to fetch Master Suds the barber.

SIMON
Master Suds? A good man: he washes the sins of the beard clean.

[Enter old Skirmish the **SOLDIER**.

SKIRMISH
How now, creatures? What's a'clock?

FRAILTY
Why, do you take us to be jacks a' th' clock-house?

SKIRMISH
I say again to you, what's a'clock?

SIMON
Truly, la, we go by the clock of our conscience. All worldly clocks we know go false, and are set by drunken sextons.

SKIRMISH
Then what's a'clock in your conscience?

[Enter **CORPORAL OATH**.

[Aside] Oh, I must break off: here comes the corporal.—Hum, hum. [To **CORPORAL OATH**] What's a'clock?

CORPORAL OATH

A'clock? Why, past seventeen.

FRAILTY [To **SIMON**]

Past seventeen! Nay, h'as met with his match now: Corporal Oath will fit him.

SKIRMISH

Thou dost not balk or baffle me, doest thou? I am a soldier. Past seventeen!

CORPORAL OATH

Ay, thou art not angry with the figures, art thou? I will prove it unto thee. Twelve and one is thirteen, I hope, two fourteen, three fifteen, four sixteen, and five seventeen: then past seventeen; I will take the dial's part in a just cause.

SKIRMISH

I say 'tis but past five then.

CORPORAL OATH

I'll swear 'tis past seventeen then. Doest thou not know numbers? Canst thou not cast?

SKIRMISH

Cast? Dost thou speak of my casting i' th' street?

CORPORAL OATH

Ay, and in the marketplace.

[They draw and fight.

SIMON

Clubs, clubs, clubs!

[**SIMON** runs in.

FRAILTY

Ay, I knew by their shuffling, clubs would be trump. Mass, here's the knave, and he can do any good upon 'em. Clubs, clubs, clubs!

[Enter **PYEBOARD. SKIRMISH** wounds **CORPORAL OATH** on the leg.

CORPORAL OATH

Oh villain, thou hast open'd a vein in my leg!

PYEBOARD

How now? For shame, for shame, put up, put up!

CORPORAL OATH

By yon blue welkin, 'twas out of my part, George, to be hurt on the leg!

[Enter **OFFICERS**.

PYEBOARD
Oh, peace now! I have a cordial here to comfort thee.

[He gives **CORPORAL OATH** the cordial, which he drinks.

OFFICER
Down with 'em, down with 'em; lay hands upon the villain!

[The **OFFICERS** seize **SKIRMISH** and **CORPORAL OATH**.

SKIRMISH
Lay hands on me?

PYEBOARD
I'll not be seen among 'em now.

[**PYEBOARD** withdraws.

CORPORAL OATH
I'm hurt, and had more need have surgeons
Lay hands upon me than rough officers!

OFFICER
Go, carry him to be dress'd then; this mutinous soldier shall along with me to prison.

[Exeunt some of the **OFFICERS** with **CORPORAL OATH**.

SKIRMISH
To prison? Where's George?

OFFICER
Away with him!

[Exeunt **OFFICERS** with **SKIRMISH**.

PYEBOARD
So,
All lights as I would wish. The amaz'd widow
Will plant me strongly now in her belief
And wonder at the virtue of my words,
For the event turns those presages from 'em
Of being mad and dumb, and begets joy
Mingled with admiration. These empty creatures,
Soldier and corporal, were but ordain'd
As instruments for me to work upon.
Now to my patient; here's his potion.

[Exit **PYEBOARD**.

SCENE II - An Apartment in the Widow's House

Enter the **WIDOW** with her two daughters **FRANK** and **MOLL**, together with **FRAILITY**.

WIDOW
Oh wondrous happiness, beyond our thoughts!
Oh lucky fair event! I think our fortunes
Were blest e'en in our cradles. We are quitted
Of all those shameful violent presages
By this rash, bleeding chance. Go, Frailty, run and know
Whether he be yet living or yet dead
That here before my door receiv'd his hurt.

FRAILTY
Madam, he was carried to the surgeon, but if he had no money when he came there, I warrant he's dead by this time.

[Exit **FRAILITY**.

FRANK
Sure that man is a rare fortune-teller: never look'd upon our hands nor upon any mark about us; a wondrous fellow, surely!

MOLL [Aside]
I am glad I have the use of my tongue yet, though of nothing else. I shall find the way to marry too, I hope, shortly.

WIDOW
Oh, where's my brother Sir Godfrey? I would he were here that I might relate to him how prophetically the cunning gentleman spoke in all things.

[Enter **SIR GODFREY** in a rage.

SIR GODFREY
Oh, my chain, my chain! I have lost my chain! Where be these villains, varlets?

WIDOW
Oh, he has lost his chain!

SIR GODFREY
My chain, my chain!

WIDOW

Brother, be patient; here me speak. You know I told you that a cunning-man told me that you should have a loss, and he has prophesied so true—

SIR GODFREY

Out! He's a villain to prophesy of the loss of my chain. 'Twas worth above three hundred crowns. Besides, 'twas my father's, my father's father's, my grandfather's huge grandfather's: I had as lief ha' lost my neck as the chain that hung about it. Oh, my chain, my chain!

WIDOW

Oh, brother, who can be guarded against a misfortune? 'Tis happy 'twas no more.

SIR GODFREY

No more! Oh goodly godly sister, would you had me lost more? My best gown too, with the cloth-of-gold lace? My holiday gaskins, and my jerkin set with pearl? No more!

WIDOW

Oh, brother, you can read—

SIR GODFREY

But I cannot read where my chain is. What strangers have been here? You let in strangers, thieves, and catchpoles. How comes it gone? There was none above with me but my tailor, and my tailor will not steal, I hope.

MOLL

No, he's afraid of a chain!

[Enter **FRAILITY**.

WIDOW

How now, sirrah? The news?

FRAILTY

Oh, mistress, he may well be call'd a corporal now, for his corpse is as dead as a cold capon's.

WIDOW

More happiness!

SIR GODFREY

Sirrah, what's this to my chain? Where's my chain, knave?

FRAILTY

Your chain, sir?

SIR GODFREY

My chain is lost, villain.

FRAILTY

I would he were hang'd in chains that has it then for me. Alas, sir, I saw none of your chain since you were hung with it yourself.

SIR GODFREY
Out, varlet! It had full three thousand links;
I have oft told it over at my prayers,
Over and over, full three thousand links.

FRAILTY
Had it so, sir? Sure it cannot be lost then; I'll put you in that comfort.

SIR GODFREY
Why? Why?

FRAILTY
Why, if your chain had so many links, it cannot choose but come to light.

[Enter **NICHOLAS**.

SIR GODFREY
Delusion! Now, long Nicholas, where's my chain?

NICHOLAS
Why, about your neck, is't not, sir?

SIR GODFREY
About my neck, varlet? My chain is lost: 'tis stole away; I'm robb'd!

WIDOW
Nay, brother, show yourself a man.

NICHOLAS
Ay, if it be lost or stole, if he would be patient, mistress, I could bring him to a cunning kinsman of mine that would fetch 't again with a sesarara.

SIR GODFREY
Canst thou? I will be patient; say, where dwells he?

NICHOLAS
Marry, he dwells now, sir, where he would not dwell and he could choose: in the Marshalsea, sir. But he's an ex'lent fellow if he were out; h'as travell'd all the world o'er, he, and been in the seven-and-twenty provinces. Why, he would make it be fetch'd, sir, if 'twere rid a thousand mile out of town.

SIR GODFREY
An admirable fellow! What lies he for?

NICHOLAS

Why, he did but rob a steward of ten groats t'other night, as any man would ha' done, and there he lies for't.

SIR GODFREY
I'll make his peace. A trifle! I'll get his pardon,
Beside a bountiful reward. I'll about it.
But fee the clerks, the justice will do much.
I will about it straight. Good sister, pardon me;
All will be well, I hope, and turn to good:
The name of conjurer has laid my blood.

[Exeunt.

SCENE III - A Street

Enter two sergeants **PUTTOCK** and **RAVENSHAW**, with Yeoman **DOGSON** to arrest the scholar, George **PYEBOARD** [who enters later].

PUTTOCK
His hostess where he lies will trust him no longer. She has feed me to arrest him, and if you will accompany me, because I know not of what nature the scholar is, whether desperate or swift, you shall share with me, Sergeant Ravenshaw. I have the good angel to arrest him.

RAVENSHAW
Troth, I'll take part with thee, then, sergeant, not for the sake of the money so much, as for the hate I bear to a scholar. Why, sergeant, 'tis natural in us, you know, to hate scholars, natural; besides, they will publish our imperfections, knaveries, and conveyances upon scaffolds and stages.

PUTTOCK
Ay, and spitefully too. Troth, I have wonder'd how the slaves could see into our breasts so much, when our doublets are button'd with pewter.

RAVENSHAW
Ay, and so close without yielding. Oh, they're parlous fellows; they will search more with their wits than a constable with all his officers.

PUTTOCK
Whist, whist, whist! Yeoman Dogson, Yeoman Dogson.

DOGSON
Ha! What says sergeant?

PUTTOCK
Is he in the 'pothecary's shop still?

DOGSON

Ay, ay.

PUTTOCK
Have an eye, have an eye.

RAVENSHAW
The best is, sergeant, if he be a true scholar, he wears no weapon, I think.

PUTTOCK
No, no, he wears no weapon.

RAVENSHAW
Mass, I am right glad of that; 't 'as put me in better heart. Nay, if I clutch him once, let me alone to drag him if he be stiff-necked. I have been one of the six myself that has dragg'd as tall men of their hands when their weapons have been gone, as ever bastinado'd a sergeant. I have done, I can tell you.

DOGSON
Sergeant Puttock, Sergeant Puttock!

PUTTOCK
Ho!

DOGSON
He's coming out single.

PUTTOCK
Peace, peace, be not too greedy; let him play a little, let him play a little. We'll jerk him up of a sudden: I ha' fish'd in my time.

RAVENSHAW
Ay, and caught many a fool, sergeant.

[Enter **PYEBOARD**.

PYEBOARD [Aside]
I parted now from Nicholas: the chain's couch'd,
And the old knight has spent his rage upon't.
The widow holds me in great admiration
For cunning art. 'Mongst joys I am e'en lost,
For my device can no way now be cross'd;
And now I must to prison to the captain,
And there—

[**RAVENSHAW** and **DOGSON** seize **PYEBOARD**.

PUTTOCK
I arrest you, sir.

PYEBOARD

Oh! I spoke truer than I was aware: I must to prison indeed.

PUTTOCK

They say you're a scholar. [**PYEBOARD** struggles.] Nay, sir! Yeoman Dogson, have care to his arms. You'll rail against sergeants and stage 'em? You['ll] tickle their vices?

PYEBOARD

Nay, use me like a gentleman; I'm little less.

PUTTOCK

You a gentleman! That's a good jest, i'faith. Can a scholar be a gentleman when a gentleman will not be a scholar? Look upon your wealthy citizens' sons, whether they be scholars or no, that are gentlemen by their fathers' trades. A scholar a gentleman!

PYEBOARD

Nay, let fortune drive all her stings into me, she cannot hurt that in me. A gentleman is accidens inseparabile to my blood.

RAVENSHAW

A rabblement! Nay, you shall have a bloody rabblement upon you, I warrant you.

PUTTOCK

Go, Yeoman Dogson, before, and enter the action i' th' Counter.

[Exit **DOGSON**.

PYEBOARD

Pray do not handle me cruelly; I'll go whither you please to have me.

PUTTOCK

Oh, he's tame; let him loose, sergeant.

PYEBOARD

Pray, at whose suit is this?

PUTTOCK

Why, at your hostess's suit where you lie, Mistress Conyburrow, for bed and board, the sum four pound five shillings and five pence.

PYEBOARD

I know the sum too true, yet I presum'd
Upon a farther day. Well, 'tis my stars,
And I must bear it now, though never harder.
I swear now my device is cross'd indeed;
Th' captain must lie by't: this is deceit's seed.

PUTTOCK

Come, come away.

PYEBOARD
Pray give me so much time as to knit my garter, and I'll away with you.

PUTTOCK
Well, we must be paid for this waiting upon you; this is no pains to attend thus.

PYEBOARD [Making to tie his garter]
I am now wretched and miserable; I shall ne'er recover of this disease. Hot iron gnaw their fists! They have struck a fever into my shoulder, which I shall ne'er shake out again, I fear me, till with a true habeas corpus the sexton remove me. Oh, if I take prison once, I shall be press'd to death with actions, but not so happy as speedily: perhaps I may be forty years a-pressing, till I be a thin, old man, that looking through the grates, men may look through me. All my means are confounded. What shall I do? Has my wit served me so long and now gives me the slip, like a train'd servant, when I have most need of it? No device to keep my poor carcass fro' these puttocks? Yes, happiness! Have I a paper about me now? Yes, too! I'll try it; it may hit. "Extremity is the touchstone unto wit." Ay, ay.

PUTTOCK
'Sfoot, how many yards are in thy garters that thou art so long a-tying of them? Come away, sir.

PYEBOARD
Troth, sergeant, I protest, you could never ha' took me at a worse time, for now at this instant I have no lawful picture about me.

PUTTOCK
'Slid, how shall we come by our fees then?

RAVENSHAW
We must have fees, sirrah.

PYEBOARD
I could ha' wish'd, i'faith, that you had took me half an hour hence for your own sake, for, I protest, if you had not cross'd me, I was going in great joy to receive five pound of a gentleman for the device of a masque here, drawn in this paper. But now, come, I must be contented; 'tis but so much lost, and answerable to the rest of my fortunes.

PUTTOCK
Why, how far hence dwells that gentleman?

RAVENSHAW
Ay, well said, sergeant; 'tis good to cast about for money.

PUTTOCK
Speak; if it be not far—

PYEBOARD
We are but a little past it: the next street behind us.

PUTTOCK

'Slid, we have waited upon you grievously already. If you'll say you'll be liberal when you ha't, give us double fees, and spend upon 's, why, we'll show you that kindness and go along with you to the gentleman.

RAVENSHAW

Ay, well said, still, sergeant; urge that.

PYEBOARD

Troth, if it will suffice, it shall be all among you; for my part I'll not pocket a penny: my hostess shall have her four pound five shillings and bate me the five pence, and the other fifteen shillings I'll spend upon you.

RAVENSHAW

Why, now thou art a good scholar.

PUTTOCK

An excellent scholar, i'faith; h'as proceeded very well alate. Come, we'll along with you.

[Exeunt **PUTTOCK** and **RAVENSHAW** with him: passing in they knock at the door with a knocker withinside.

SCENE IV - A Gallery in a Gentleman's House

Enter a **SERVANT**.

SERVANT

Who knocks? Who's at door? We had need of a porter.

PYEBOARD [Within]

A few friends here.

[The **SERVANT** opens the door. Enter **PYEBOARD, PUTTOCK, RAVENSHAW,** and **DOGSON**.

Pray, is the gentleman your master within?

SERVANT

Yes; is your business to him?

PYEBOARD

Ay, he knows it when he sees me; I pray you, have you forgot me?

SERVANT

Ay, by my troth, sir. Pray come near; I'll in and tell him of you. Please you to walk here in the gallery till he comes.

PYEBOARD
We will attend his worship.

[Exit **SERVANT**.

[Aside] Worship, I think, for so much the posts at his door should signify, and the fair coming-in, and the wicket, else I neither knew him nor his worship; but 'tis happiness he is within doors, whatsoe'er he be. If he be not too much a formal citizen, he may do me good.—Sergeant and yeoman, how do you like this house? Is't not most wholesomely plotted?

RAVENSHAW
Troth, prisoner, an exceeding fine house.

PYEBOARD
Yet I wonder how he should forget me, [Aside] for he never knew me.—No matter; what is forgot in you will be remember'd in your master. A pretty, comfortable room this, methinks; you have no such rooms in prison now?

PUTTOCK
Oh, dog-holes to't!

PYEBOARD
Dog-holes indeed. I can tell you, I have great hope to have my chamber here shortly, nay, and diet too, for he's the most free-heartedst gentleman where he takes; you would little think it. And what a fine gallery were here for me to walk and study and make verses.

PUTTOCK
Oh, it stands very pleasantly for a scholar.

[Enter **GENTLEMAN**.

PYEBOARD
Look what maps, and pictures, and devices, and things, neatly, delicately. Mass, here he comes; he should be a gentleman: I like his beard well. All happiness to your worship!

GENTLEMAN
You're kindly welcome, sir.

PUTTOCK [Aside to **RAVENSHAW**]
A simple salutation.

RAVENSHAW [Aside to **PUTTOCK**]
Mass, it seems the gentleman makes great account of him.

PYEBOARD
I have the thing here for you, sir. [Aside to the **GENTLEMAN**] I beseech you, conceal me, sir; I'm undone else.—

[Aloud, showing him a paper.

I have the masque here for you, sir; look you, sir. [Aside to him] I beseech your worship, first pardon my rudeness, for my extremes make me bolder than I would be. I am a poor gentleman and a scholar, and now most unfortunately fall'n into the fangs of unmerciful officers, arrested for debt, which, though small, I am not able to compass, by reason I'm destitute of lands, money, and friends; so that if I fall into the hungry swallow of the prison, I am like utterly to perish, and with fees and extortions be pinch'd clean to the bone. Now, if ever pity had interest in the blood of a gentleman, I beseech you vouchsafe but to favour that means of my escape, which I have already thought upon.

GENTLEMAN
Go forward.

PUTTOCK [Aside to RAVENSHAW]
I warrant he likes it rarely.

PYEBOARD [Aside to the GENTLEMAN]
In the plunge of my extremities, being giddy and doubtful what to do, at last it was put into my labouring thoughts to make happy use of this paper, and to blear their unletter'd eyes, I told them there was a device for a masque drawn in't, and that, but for their interception, I was going to a gentleman to receive my reward for't. They, greedy at this word, and hoping to make purchase of me, offered their attendance to go along with me. My hap was to make bold with your door, sir, which my thoughts show'd me the most fairest and comfortablest entrance, and I hope I have happened right upon understanding and pity. May it please your good worship then but to uphold my device, which is to let one of your men put me out at a back door, and I shall be bound to your worship forever.

GENTLEMAN
By my troth, an excellent device.

PUTTOCK [Aside to **RAVENSHAW**]
An excellent device, he says; he likes it wonderfully.

GENTLEMAN
A' my faith, I never heard a better.

RAVENSHAW [Aside to **PUTTOCK**]
Hark, he swears he never heard a better, sergeant.

PUTTOCK [Aside to **RAVENSHAW**]
Oh, there's no talk on't: he's an excellent scholar, especially for a masque.

GENTLEMAN
Give me your paper, your device; I was never better pleas'd in all my life. Good wit, brave wit, finely wrought! Come in, sir, and receive your money, sir.

PYEBOARD
I'll follow your good worship.

[Exit **GENTLEMAN**.

You heard how he lik'd it now?

PUTTOCK
Puh, we know he could not choose but like it. Go thy ways; thou art a witty, fine fellow, i'faith. Thou shalt discourse it to us at tavern anon, wilt thou?

PYEBOARD
Ay, ay, that I will. Look, sergeants, here are maps and pretty toys: be doing in the meantime; I shall quickly have told out the money, you know.

PUTTOCK
Go, go, little villain; fetch thy chink. I begin to love thee; I'll be drunk tonight in thy company.

PYEBOARD [Aside]
This gentleman I well may call a part
Of my salvation in these earthly evils,
For he has sav'd me from three hungry devils.

[Exit George **PYEBOARD**.

PUTTOCK [Looking at a map]
Sirrah sergeant, these maps are pretty painted things, but I could ne'er fancy 'em yet; methinks they're too busy, and full of circles and conjurations. They say all the world's in one of them, but I could ne'er find the Counter in the Poultry.

RAVENSHAW
I think so; how could you find it, for you know it stands behind the houses.

DOGSON
Mass, that's true; then we must look a' th' backside for't.

[He turns the map over.]

'Sfoot, here's nothing; all's bare.

RAVENSHAW
I warrant thee that stands for the Counter, for you know there's a company of bare fellows there.

PUTTOCK
Faith, like enough, sergeant; I never mark'd so much before. Sirrah sergeant and yeoman, I should love these maps out a' cry now if we could see men peep out of door in 'em. Oh, we might have 'em in a morning to our breakfast so finely and ne'er knock our heels to the ground a whole day for 'em.

RAVENSHAW

Ay, marry, sir, I'd buy one then myself. But this talk is by the way. Where shall's sup tonight? Five pound receiv'd: let's talk of that. I have a trick worth all. You two shall bear him to th' tavern whilst I go close with his hostess and work out of her. I know she would be glad of the sum to finger money, because she knows 'tis but a desperate debt and full of hazard. What will you say if I bring it to pass that the hostess shall be contented with one-half for all and we to share t'other fifty shillings, bullies?

PUTTOCK
Why, I would call thee king of sergeants, and thou should'st be chronicled in the Counter-book forever.

RAVENSHAW
Well, put it to me; we'll make a night on't, i'faith.

DOGSON
'Sfoot, I think he receives more money, he stays so long.

PUTTOCK
He tarries long indeed. Maybe I can tell you, upon the good liking on't, the gentleman may prove more bountiful.

RAVENSHAW
That would be rare; we'll search him.

PUTTOCK
Nay, be sure of it, we'll search him and make him light enough.

[Enter the **GENTLEMAN**.

RAVENSHAW
Oh, here comes the gentleman. By your leave, sir.

GENTLEMAN
God you good den, sirs. Would you speak with me?

PUTTOCK
No, not with your worship, sir; only we are bold to stay for a friend of ours that went in with your worship.

GENTLEMAN
Who? Not the scholar?

PUTTOCK
Yes, e'en he, and it please your worship.

GENTLEMAN
Did he make you stay for him? He did you wrong then; why, I can assure you he's gone above an hour ago.

RAVENSHAW

How, sir!

GENTLEMAN
I paid him his money and my man told me he went out at back door.

PUTTOCK
Back door?

GENTLEMAN
Why, what's the matter?

PUTTOCK
He was our prisoner, sir; we did arrest him.

GENTLEMAN
What? He was not! You, the sheriff's officers? You were to blame then. Why did not you make known to me as much? I could have kept him for you. I protest, he receiv'd all of me in Britain gold of the last coining.

RAVENSHAW
Vengeance dog him with't!

PUTTOCK
'Sfoot, has he gull'd us so?

DOGSON
Where shall we sup now, sergeants?

PUTTOCK
Sup, Simon, now! Eat porridge for a month! Well, we cannot impute it to any lack of good will in your worship. You did but as another would have done. 'Twas our hard fortunes to miss the purchase; but if e'er we clutch him again, the Counter shall charm him.

RAVENSHAW
The Hole shall rot him!

DOGSON
Amen.

[Exeunt **PUTTOCK**, **RAVENSHAW**, and **DOGSON**.

GENTLEMAN
So;
Vex out your lungs without doors. I am proud
It was my hap to help him. It fell fit;
He went not empty neither for his wit.
Alas, poor wretch, I could not blame his brain
To labour his delivery to be free

From their unpitying fangs. I'm glad it stood
Within my power to do a scholar good.

[Exit.

SCENE V – Captain Idle's Cell in the Marshalsea Prison

Enter in the prison, meeting, George **PYEBOARD** and **CAPTAIN IDLE**, George coming in muffled.

CAPTAIN IDLE
How now! Who's that? What are you?

PYEBOARD [Showing his face]
The same that I should be, captain.

CAPTAIN IDLE
George Pyeboard? Honest George? Why cam'st thou in half-fac'd, muffled so?

PYEBOARD
Oh, captain, I thought we should ne'er ha' laugh'd again, never spent frolic hour again.

CAPTAIN IDLE
Why? Why?

PYEBOARD
I, coming to prepare thee, and with news
As happy as thy quick delivery,
Was trac'd out by the scent: arrested, captain.

CAPTAIN IDLE
Arrested, George?

PYEBOARD
Arrested. Guess, guess,
How many dogs do you think I'd upon me?

CAPTAIN IDLE
Dogs? I say, I know not.

PYEBOARD
Almost as many as George Stone the bear: three at once, three at once!

CAPTAIN IDLE
How didst thou shake 'em off then?

PYEBOARD

The time is busy and calls upon our wits.
Let it suffice,
Here I stand safe and scap'd by miracle;
Some other hour shall tell thee, when we'll steep
Our eyes in laughter. Captain, my device
Leans to thy happiness, for ere the day
Be spent to th' girdle, thou shalt be set free.
The corporal's in his first sleep, the chain is miss'd,
Thy kinsman has express'd thee, and the old knight
With palsy hams now labours thy release.
What rests is all in thee: to conjure, captain.

CAPTAIN IDLE

Conjure! 'Sfoot, George, you know, the devil a-conjuring I can conjure!

PYEBOARD

The devil a-conjuring? Nay, by my fay, I'd not have thee do so much, captain, as the devil a-conjuring.

[Giving him a conjuring circle]

Look here, I ha' brought thee a circle ready character'd and all.

CAPTAIN IDLE

'Sfoot, George, art in thy right wits? Dost know what thou sayst? Why dost talk to a captain a' conjuring? Didst thou ever hear of a captain conjure in thy life? Dost call't a circle? 'Tis too wide a thing, methinks; had it been a lesser circle, then I knew what to have done.

PYEBOARD

Why, every fool knows that, captain. Nay then, I'll not cog with you captain: if you'll stay and hang the next sessions, you may.

CAPTAIN IDLE

No, by my faith, George. Come, come; let's to conjuring, let's to conjuring.

PYEBOARD

But if you look to be releas'd, as my wits have took pain to work it and all means wrought to farther it; besides, to put crowns in your purse, to make you a man of better hopes. And whereas before you were a captain or poor soldier, to make you now a commander of rich fools, which is truly the only best purchase peace can allow you, safer than highways, heath, or cony-groves, and yet a far better booty, for your greatest thieves are never hang'd, never hang'd, for, why, they're wise and cheat within doors; and we geld fools of more money in one night than your false-tail'd gelding will purchase in a twelve-month's running, which confirms the old beldam's saying, "He's wisest that keeps himself warmest," that is, he that robs by a good fire.

CAPTAIN IDLE

Well opened, i'faith, George; thou hast pull'd that saying out of the husk.

PYEBOARD

Captain Idle, 'tis no time now to delude or delay; the old knight will be here suddenly. I'll perfect you, direct you, tell you the trick on't: 'tis nothing.

CAPTAIN IDLE
'Sfoot, George, I know not what to say to't. Conjure? I shall be hang'd ere I can conjure.

PYEBOARD
Nay, tell not me of that, captain; you'll ne'er conjure after you're hang'd, I warrant you. Look you, sir, a parlous matter, sure. First to spread your circle upon the ground with a little conjuring ceremony, as I'll have an hackney-man's wand silver'd o'er a' purpose for you; then arriving in the circle with a huge word and a great trample, as for instance: have you never seen a stalking, stamping player that will raise a tempest with his tongue and thunder with his heels?

CAPTAIN IDLE
Oh, yes, yes, yes; often, often!

PYEBOARD
Why, be like such a one, for anything will blear the old knight's eyes; for you must note that he'll ne'er dare to venture into the room, only perhaps peep fearfully through the keyhole, to see how the play goes forward.

CAPTAIN IDLE
Well, I may go about it when I will, but mark the end on't: I shall but shame myself, i'faith, George. Speak big words, and stamp and stare, and he look in at keyhole! Why, the very thought of that would make me laugh outright and spoil all! Nay, I'll tell thee, George, when I apprehend a thing once, I am of such a laxative laughter, that if the devil himself stood by, I should laugh in his face.

PYEBOARD
Puh! That's but the babe of a man and may easily be hush'd, as to think upon some disaster, some sad misfortune, as the death of thy father i' the country.

CAPTAIN IDLE
'Sfoot, that would be the more to drive me into such an ecstasy that I should ne'er lin laughing.

PYEBOARD
Why, then think upon going to hanging else.

CAPTAIN IDLE
Mass, that's well remembered. Now I'll do well, I warrant thee; ne'er fear me now. But how shall I do, George, for boisterous words and horrible names?

PYEBOARD
Puh! Any fustian invocations, captain, will serve as well as the best, so you rant them out well; or you may go to a 'pothecary's shop and take all the words from the boxes.

CAPTAIN IDLE

Troth, and you say true, George; there's strange words enow to raise a hundred quacksalvers, though they be ne'er so poor when they begin. But here lies the fear on't: how if in this false conjuration a true devil should pop up indeed?

PYEBOARD
A true devil, captain? Why, there was ne'er such a one. Nay, faith, he that has this place is as false a knave as our last churchwarden.

CAPTAIN IDLE
Then he's false enough a' conscience, i'faith, George.

[The cry at Marshalsea.

PRISONERS [cry within]
Good gentlemen over the way, send your relief! Good gentlemen over the way! Good Sir Godfrey!

PYEBOARD
He's come, he's come.

[Enter **SIR GODFREY**, **EDMOND**, and **NICHOLAS**.

NICHOLAS
Master, that's my kinsman yonder in the buff-jerkin. Kinsman, that's my master yonder i' th' taffety hat. Pray salute him entirely.

[**SIR GODFREY** and **CAPTAIN IDLE** salute, and **PYEBOARD** salutes Master **EDMOND**.

SIR GODFREY [Taking **CAPTAIN IDLE** aside]
Now, my friend—

PYEBOARD
May I partake your name, sir?

EDMOND
My name is Master Edmond.

PYEBOARD
Master Edmond? Are you not a Welshman, sir?

EDMOND
A Welshman? Why?

PYEBOARD
Because Master is your Christian name and Edmond your surname.

EDMOND
Oh, no, I have more names at home; Master Edmond Plus is my full name at length.

PYEBOARD
Oh, cry you mercy, sir!

CAPTAIN IDLE
I understand that you are my kinsman's good master, and in regard of that, the best of my skill is at your service. But had you fortun'd a mere stranger and made no means to me by acquaintance, I should have utterly denied to have been the man, both by reason of the act pass'd in parliament against conjurers and witches, as also because I would not have my art vulgar, trite, and common.

SIR GODFREY
I much commend your care therein, good captain conjurer, and that I will be sure to have it private enough, you shall do't in my sister's house; mine own house I may call it, for both our charges therein are proportion'd.

CAPTAIN IDLE
Very good, sir. What may I call your loss, sir?

SIR GODFREY
Oh, you may call 't a great loss, a grievous loss, sir, as goodly a chain of gold, though I say it, that wore it. How sayst thou, Nicholas?

NICHOLAS
Oh, 'twas as delicious a chain of gold, kinsman, you know—

SIR GODFREY
You know? Did you know't, captain?

CAPTAIN IDLE [Aside]
Trust a fool with secrets!—Sir, he may say I know. His meaning is, because my art is such, that by it I may gather a knowledge of all things.

SIR GODFREY
Ay, very true.

CAPTAIN IDLE [Aside]
A pox of all fools! The excuse stuck upon my tongue like ship-pitch upon a mariner's gown, not to come off in haste.—Berlady, knight, to lose such a fair chain of gold were a foul loss. Well, I can put you in this good comfort on't: if it be between heaven and earth, knight, I'll ha't for you.

SIR GODFREY
A wonderful conjurer! Oh, ay, 'tis between heaven and earth, I warrant you; it cannot go out of the realm. I know 'tis somewhere above the earth—

CAPTAIN IDLE [Aside]
Ay, nigher the earth than thou wotst on.

SIR GODFREY
For, first, my chain was rich, and no rich thing shall enter into heaven, you know.

NICHOLAS
And as for the devil, master, he has no need on't, for you know he has a great chain of his own.

SIR GODFREY
Thou sayst true, Nicholas, but he has put off that now; that lies by him.

CAPTAIN IDLE
Faith, knight, in few words, I presume so much upon the power of my art that I could warrant your chain again.

SIR GODFREY
Oh, dainty captain!

CAPTAIN IDLE
Marry, it will cost me much sweat; I were better go to sixteen hothouses.

SIR GODFREY
Ay, good man, I warrant thee.

CAPTAIN IDLE
Beside great vexation of kidney and liver.

NICHOLAS
Oh, 'twill tickle you hereabouts, cousin, because you have not been used to't.

SIR GODFREY
No? Have you not been us'd to't, captain?

CAPTAIN IDLE [Aside]
Plague of all fools still!—Indeed, knight, I have not us'd it a good while, and therefore 'twill strain me so much the more, you know.

SIR GODFREY
Oh, it will, it will.

CAPTAIN IDLE [Aside]
What plunges he puts me to! Were not this knight a fool, I had been twice spoil'd now. That captain's worse than accurs'd that has an ass to his kinsman. 'Sfoot, I fear he will drivel 't out before I come to't!—Now, sir to come to the point indeed: you see I stick here in the jaw of the Marshalsea and cannot do't.

SIR GODFREY
Tut, tut, I know thy meaning: thou would'st say thou'rt a prisoner; I tell thee thou'rt none.

CAPTAIN IDLE
How, none? Why, is not this the Marshalsea?

SIR GODFREY

Woult hear me speak? I heard of thy rare conjuring:
My chain was lost; I sweat for thy release
As thou shalt do the like at home for me.
Keeper!

[Enter **KEEPER**.

KEEPER
Sir.

SIR GODFREY
Speak, is not this man free?

KEEPER
Yes, at his pleasure, sir, the fees discharg'd.

SIR GODFREY
Go, go; I'll discharge them, I.

KEEPER
I thank your worship.

[Exit **KEEPER**.

CAPTAIN IDLE
Now, trust me, y'are a dear knight! Kindness unexpected! Oh, there's nothing to a free gentleman! I will conjure you, sir, till froth come through my buff-jerkin.

SIR GODFREY
Nay, then thou shalt not pass with so little a bounty, for at the first sight of my chain again, forty fine angels shall appear unto thee.

CAPTAIN IDLE
'Twill be a glorious show, i'faith, knight, a very fine show. But are all these of your own house? Are you sure of that, sir?

SIR GODFREY
Ay, ay; no, no. What's he yonder talking with my wild nephew? Pray heaven he give him good counsel.

CAPTAIN IDLE
Who, he? He's a rare friend of mine: an admirable fellow, knight, the finest fortune-teller.

SIR GODFREY
Oh! 'Tis he indeed that came to my lady sister and foretold the loss of my chain; I am not angry with him now, for I see 'twas my fortune to lose it. By your leave, master fortune-teller, I had a glimpse on you at home, at my sister's the widow's; there you prophesied of the loss of a chain; simply though I stand here, I was he that lost it.

PYEBOARD
Was is you, sir?

EDMOND
A' my troth, nuncle, he's the rarest fellow; h'as told me my fortune so right! I find it so right to my nature.

SIR GODFREY
What is't? God send it a good one.

EDMOND
Oh, 'tis a passing good one, nuncle, for he says I shall prove such an excellent gamester in my time that I shall spend all faster than my father got it.

SIR GODFREY
There's a fortune indeed.

EDMOND
Nay, it hits my humour so pat.

SIR GODFREY
Ay, that will be the end on't. Will the curse of the beggar prevail so much that the son shall consume that foolishly which the father got craftily? Ay, ay, ay; 'twill, 'twill, 'twill.

PYEBOARD
Stay, stay, stay.

[**PYEBOARD** opens an almanac and takes the **CAPTAIN** aside.

CAPTAIN IDLE
Turn over, George.

PYEBOARD
June, July; here, July: that's this month. Sunday thirteen, yesterday fourteen, today fifteen.

CAPTAIN IDLE
Look quickly for the fifteen day. If within the compass of these two days there would be some boisterous storm or other, it would be the best; I'd defer him off till then. Some tempest, and it be thy will.

PYEBOARD
Here's the fifteen day. [Reading] "Hot and fair."

CAPTAIN IDLE
Puh! Would 't 'ad been hot and foul.

PYEBOARD
The sixteen day, that's tomorrow. [Reading] "The morning for the most part fair and pleasant"—

CAPTAIN IDLE
No luck.

PYEBOARD
"But about high noon, lightning and thunder."

CAPTAIN IDLE
Lightning and thunder? Admirable! Best of all! I'll conjure tomorrow just at high noon, George.

PYEBOARD
Happen but true tomorrow, almanac, and I'll give thee leave to lie all the year after.

CAPTAIN IDLE [To **SIR GODFREY**]
Sir, I must crave your patience to bestow this day upon me, that I may furnish myself strongly. I sent a spirit into Lancashire t'other day to fetch back a knave drover, and I look for his return this evening. Tomorrow morning my friend here and I will come and breakfast with you.

SIR GODFREY
Oh, you shall be both most welcome.

CAPTAIN IDLE
And about noon, without fail, I purpose to conjure.

SIR GODFREY
Mid-noon will be a fine time for you.

EDMOND
Conjuring? Do you mean to conjure at our house tomorrow, sir?

CAPTAIN IDLE
Marry, do I, sir; 'tis my intent, young gentleman.

EDMOND
By my troth, I'll love you while I live for't. Oh, rare! Nicholas, we shall have conjuring tomorrow.

NICHOLAS
Puh! Ay, I could ha' told you of that.

CAPTAIN IDLE [Aside]
Law, he could ha' told him of that! Fool, coxcomb, could ye?

EDMOND
Do you hear, sir? I desire more acquaintance on you. You shall earn some money of me, now I know you can conjure. But can you fetch any that is lost?

CAPTAIN IDLE
Oh, anything that's lost.

EDMOND

Why, look you, sir, I tell 't you as a friend and a conjurer. I should marry a 'pothecary's daughter, and 'twas told me she lost her maidenhead at Stony-Stratford; now if you'll do but so much as conjure for't, and make all whole again—

CAPTAIN IDLE

That I will, sir.

EDMOND

By my troth, I thank you, la!

CAPTAIN IDLE

A little merry with your sister's son, sir.

SIR GODFREY

Oh, a simple young man, very simple. Come, captain, and you, sir; we'll e'en part with a gallon of wine till tomorrow breakfast.

PYEBOARD, CAPTAIN IDLE

Troth, agreed, sir.

[Exit **SIR GODFREY** and **EDMOND**.

NICHOLAS

Kinsman, scholar.

PYEBOARD

Why, now thou art a good knave, worth a hundred Brownists.

NICHOLAS

Am I indeed, la? I thank you truly, la.

[Exeunt.

ACT IV

SCENE I - A Room in the Widow's House

Enter **MOLL** and **SIR JOHN PENNYDUB**.

SIR JOHN PENNYDUB

But I hope you will not serve a knight so, gentlewoman, will you? To cashier him and cast him off at your pleasure! What, do you think I was dubb'd for nothing? No, by my faith, lady's daughter.

MOLL

Pray, Sir John Pennydub, let it be deferr'd awhile. I have as big a heart to marry as you can have, but as the fortune-teller told me—

SIR JOHN PENNYDUB
Pox a' th' fortune-teller! Would Derrick had been his fortune seven years ago to cross my love thus! Did he know what case I was in? Why, this is able to make a man drown himself in's father's fishpond!

MOLL
And then he told me moreover, Sir John, that the breach of it kept my father in purgatory.

SIR JOHN PENNYDUB
In purgatory! Why, let him purge out his heart there; what have we to do with that? There's physicians enow there to cast his water; is that any matter to us? How can he hinder our love? Why, let him be hang'd now he's dead. Well, have I rid post day and night to bring you merry news of my father's death, and now—

MOLL
Thy father's death? Is the old farmer dead?

SIR JOHN PENNYDUB
As dead as his barn door, Moll.

MOLL
And you'll keep you word with me now, Sir John, that I shall have my coach and my coachman?

SIR JOHN PENNYDUB
Ay, faith.

MOLL
And two white horses with black feathers to draw it?

SIR JOHN PENNYDUB
Two.

MOLL
A guarded lackey to run before it and pied liveries to come trashing after 't?

SIR JOHN PENNYDUB
Thou shalt, Moll.

MOLL
And to let me have money in my purse to go whither I will.

SIR JOHN PENNYDUB
All this.

MOLL
Then come; whatsoe'er comes on't, we'll be made sure together before the maids a' the kitchen.

[Exeunt.

SCENE II - Another Room in the Widow's House

Enter **WIDOW** with her eldest daughter **FRANK**, and **FRAILITY**.

WIDOW
How now? Where's my brother Sir Godfrey? Went he forth this morning?

FRAILTY
Oh, no, madam; he's above at breakfast, with, sir reverence, a conjurer.

WIDOW
A conjurer! What manner a' fellow is he?

FRAILTY
Oh, a wondrous rare fellow, mistress, very strongly made upward, for he goes in a buff-jerkin. He says he will fetch Sir Godfrey's chain again if it hang between heaven and earth.

WIDOW
What! He will not! Then he's an ex'lent fellow, I warrant. How happy were that woman to be blest with such a husband! A man a' cunning! How does he look, Frailty? Very swartly, I warrant, with black beard, scorch'd cheeks, and smoky eyebrows.

FRAILTY
Fooh, he's neither smoke-dried, nor scorch'd, nor black, nor nothing. I tell you, madam, he looks as fair to see to as one of us. I do not think but if you saw him once, you'd take him to be a Christian.

FRANK
So fair and yet so cunning! That's to be wonder'd at, mother.

[Enter **SIR OLIVER** Muckhill and **SIR ANDREW** Tipstaff.

SIR OLIVER
Bless you, sweet lady.

SIR ANDREW
And you, fair mistress.

[Exit **FRAILITY**.

WIDOW
Coads, what do you mean, gentlemen? Fie, did I not give you your answers?

SIR OLIVER

Sweet lady.

WIDOW
Well, I will not stick with you now for a kiss;
Daughter, kiss the gentleman for once.

FRANK
Yes, forsooth.

[She kisses **SIR ANDREW**.

SIR ANDREW
I'm proud of such a favour.

WIDOW
Truly, la, Sir Oliver, y'are much to blame to come again when you know my mind, so well deliver'd as widow could deliver a thing.

SIR OLIVER
But I expect a farther comfort, lady.

WIDOW
Why, la, you now! Did I not desire you to put off your suit quite and clean when you came to me again? How say you? Did I not?

SIR OLIVER
But the sincere love which my heart bears you—

WIDOW
Go to, I'll cut you off. And, Sir Oliver, to put you in comfort afar off, my fortune is read me; I must marry again.

SIR OLIVER
Oh, blest fortune!

WIDOW
But not as long as I can choose. Nay, I'll hold out well.

SIR OLIVER
Yet are my hopes now fairer.

[Enter **FRAILITY**.

FRAILTY
Oh, madam, madam!

WIDOW
How now? What's the haste?

[**FRAILITY** whispers to her.

SIR ANDREW
Faith, Mistress Frances, I'll maintain you gallantly. I'll bring you to court, wean you among the fair society of ladies, poor kinswomen of mine, in cloth of silver; beside, you shall have your monkey, your parrot, your muskcat, and your piss, piss, piss.

FRANK
It will do very well.

WIDOW [Aside]
What, does he mean to conjure here then? How shall I do to be rid of these knights?—Please you, gentlemen, to walk a while i' th' garden, go gather a pink or a gilly-flower.

SIR OLIVER, SIR ANDREW
With all our hearts, lady, and count us favour'd.

[Exeunt **SIR ANDREW, SIR OLIVER**, and **FRAILITY**. The **WIDOW** and **FRANK** enter the adjoining room.

SIR GODFREY [Within]
Step in, Nicholas; look, is the coast clear?

NICHOLAS [Within]
Oh, as clear as a cat's eye, sir.

SIR GODFREY [Within]
Then enter, captain conjurer!

[Enter **SIR GODFREY, CAPTAIN IDLE, PYEBOARD, EDMOND, NICHOLAS**.

Now, how like you your room, sir?

CAPTAIN IDLE
Oh, wonderful convenient.

EDMOND
I can tell you, captain, simply though it lies here, 'tis the fairest room in my mother's house; as dainty a room to conjure in, methinks. Why, you may bid I cannot tell how many devils welcome in't; my father has had twenty here at once.

PYEBOARD
What! Devils?

EDMOND
Devils! No, deputies, and the wealthiest men he could get.

SIR GODFREY

Nay, put by your chats now; fall to your business roundly: the fescue of the dial is upon the crisscross of noon. But, oh, hear me, captain: a qualm comes o'er my stomach.

CAPTAIN IDLE
Why, what's the matter, sir?

SIR GODFREY
Oh, how if the devil should prove a knave and tear the hangings?

CAPTAIN IDLE
Fuh! I warrant you, Sir Godfrey.

EDMOND
Ay, nuncle, or spit fire upo' th' ceiling?

SIR GODFREY
Very true too, for 'tis but thin plaster'd and 'twill quickly take hold a' the laths; and if he chance to spit downward too, he will burn all the boards.

CAPTAIN IDLE
My life for yours, Sir Godfrey.

SIR GODFREY
My sister is very curious and dainty o'er this room, I can tell you, and therefore if he must needs spit, I pray desire him to spit i' th' chimney.

PYEBOARD
Why, assure you, Sir Godfrey, he shall not be brought up with so little manners to spit and spawl a' th' floor.

SIR GODFREY
Why, I thank you, good captain; pray have a care.

[**CAPTAIN IDLE** lays out his conjuring circle.]

Ay, fall to your circle; we'll not trouble you, I warrant you. Come, we'll into the next room, and because we'll be sure to keep him out there, we'll bar up the door with some of the godly's zealous works.

EDMOND
That will be a fine device, nuncle, and because the ground shall be as holy as the door, I'll tear two or three rosaries in pieces and strew the leaves about the chamber.

[Thunders.

Oh! The devil already!

[Runs in with **SIR GODFREY** and **NICHOLAS**.

PYEBOARD
'Sfoot, captain, speak somewhat for shame: it lightens and thunders before thou wilt begin. Why, when!

CAPTAIN IDLE
Pray, peace, George! Thou'lt make me laugh anon and spoil all.

[Lightning and thunder.

PYEBOARD
Oh, now it begins again; now, now, now, captain!

CAPTAIN IDLE [Aloud, stamping up and down]
Rumbos! Ragdayon, pur, pur, colucundrion, hois-plois!

SIR GODFREY [through the keyhole, within]
Oh, admirable conjurer! H'as fetch'd thunder already.

PYEBOARD
Hark, hark! Again, captain.

CAPTAIN IDLE
Benjamino! Gaspois! Kay! Gosgothoteron! Umbrois!

SIR GODFREY [Within]
Oh, I would the devil would come away quickly; he has no conscience to put a man to such pain!

PYEBOARD
Again!

CAPTAIN IDLE
Flowste! Kakopumpos! Dragone! Leloomenos! Hodge-podge!

PYEBOARD
Well said, captain.

SIR GODFREY [Within]
So long a-coming? Oh, would I had ne'er begun 't now, for I fear me these roaring tempests will destroy all the fruits of the earth and tread upon my corn—[thunder] oh!—i' th' country!

CAPTAIN IDLE
Gog de gog, hobgoblin, hunks, hounslow, hockley te combe park!

WIDOW [Within]
Oh, brother, brother, what a tempest's i' th' garden! Sure there's some conjuration abroad.

SIR GODFREY [Within]
'Tis at home, sister!

PYEBOARD
By and by I'll step in, captain.

CAPTAIN IDLE
Nunc! Nunc! Rip-gaskins, ipis, drip-dropite!

SIR GODFREY [Within]
He drips and drops, poor man; alas, alas!

PYEBOARD
Now I come.

CAPTAIN IDLE
O sulphure sootface—

PYEBOARD [Aloud]
Arch-conjurer, what wouldst thou with me?

SIR GODFREY [Within]
Oh, the devil, sister, i' th' dining-chamber! Sing, sister; I warrant you that will keep him out: quickly, quickly, quickly!

PYEBOARD [To **CAPTAIN IDLE**]
So, so, so, I'll release thee. Enough, captain, enough; allow us some time to laugh a little: they're shuddering and shaking by this time as if an earthquake were in their kidneys.

CAPTAIN IDLE
Sirrah George, how was't, how was't? Did I do't well enough?

PYEBOARD
Woult believe me, captain? Better than any conjurer, for here was no harm in this and yet their horrible expectation satisfied well. You were much beholding to thunder and lightning at this time; it grac'd you well, I can tell you.

CAPTAIN IDLE
I must needs say so, George. Sirrah, if we could ha' convey'd hither cleanly a cracker or a fire-wheel, 't 'ad been admirable.

PYEBOARD
Blurt, blurt! There's nothing remains to put thee to pain now, captain.

CAPTAIN IDLE
Pain? I protest, George, my heels are sorer than a Whitsun morris-dancer's.

PYEBOARD
All's past now; only to reveal that the chain's i' th' garden, where thou know'st it has lain these two days.

CAPTAIN IDLE

But I fear that fox Nicholas has reveal'd it already.

PYEBOARD
Fear not, captain; you must put it to th' venture now. Nay, 'tis time; call upon 'em. Take pity on 'em, for I believe some of 'em are in a pitiful case by this time.

CAPTAIN IDLE
Sir Godfrey? Nicholas, kinsman! 'Sfoot, they're fast at it still, George! Sir Godfrey!

SIR GODFREY [Within]
Oh, is that the devil's voice? How comes he to know my name?

CAPTAIN IDLE
Fear not, Sir Godfrey; all's quieted!

[Enter **SIR GODFREY**, the **WIDOW, FRANK**, and **NICHOLAS**.

SIR GODFREY
What, is he laid?

CAPTAIN IDLE
Laid, and has newly dropp'd your chain i' th' garden.

SIR GODFREY
I' th' garden? In our garden?

CAPTAIN IDLE
Your garden.

SIR GODFREY
Oh, sweet conjurer! Whereabouts there?

CAPTAIN IDLE
Look well about a bank of rosemary.

SIR GODFREY
Sister, the rosemary bank. Come, come; there's my chain, he says.

WIDOW
Oh, happiness; run, run!

[Exeunt **WIDOW, SIR GODFREY, FRANK**, and **NICHOLAS**.

EDMOND [Within]
Captain conjurer?

CAPTAIN IDLE
Who? Master Edmond?

EDMOND [Within]
Ay, Master Edmond. May I come in safely without danger, think you?

CAPTAIN IDLE
Fuh, long ago; 'tis all as 'twas at first.
Fear nothing; pray come near.

[Enter **EDMOND**.]

How now, man?

EDMOND
Oh, this room's mightily hot, i'faith! 'Slid, my shirt sticks to my belly already! What a steam the rogue has left behind him! Foh! This room must be air'd, gentlemen: it smells horribly of brimstone; let's open the window.

PYEBOARD
Faith, Master Edmond, 'tis but your conceit.

EDMOND
I would you could make me believe that, i'faith. Why, do you think I cannot smell his savour from another? Yet I take it kindly from you because you would not put me in a fear, i'faith. A' my troth, I shall love you for this the longest day of my life.

CAPTAIN IDLE
Puh, 'tis nothing, sir; love me when you see more.

EDMOND
Mass, now I remember, I'll look whether he has singed the hangings or no.

PYEBOARD [Aside to **CAPTAIN IDLE**]
Captain, to entertain a little sport till they come, make him believe you'll charm him invisible. He's apt to admire anything, you see. Let me alone to give force to't.

CAPTAIN IDLE [Aside to **PYEBOARD**]
Go; retire to yonder end then.

[**PYEBOARD** retires to the far end of the room.

EDMOND
I protest you are a rare fellow, are you not?

CAPTAIN IDLE
Oh, Master Edmond, you know but the least part of me yet. Why, now at this instant I could but flourish my wand thrice o'er your head and charm you invisible.

EDMOND

What? You could not! Make me walk invisible, man! I should laugh at that, i'faith. Troth, I'll requite your kindness, and you'll do't, good captain conjurer.

CAPTAIN IDLE
Nay, I should hardly deny you such a small kindness, Master Edmond Plus. Why, look you, sir, 'tis no more but this—[waving his wand],—and thus, and again, and now y'are invisible.

EDMOND
Am I, i'faith? Who would think it?

CAPTAIN IDLE
You see the fortune-teller yonder at farther end a' th' chamber. Go toward him; do what you will with him: he shall ne'er find you.

EDMOND
Say you so? I'll try that, i'faith.

[**EDMOND** justles him.

PYEBOARD
How now, captain? Who's that justled me?

CAPTAIN IDLE
Justled you? I saw nobody.

EDMOND [Aside to **CAPTAIN IDLE**]
Ha, ha, ha! Say 'twas a spirit.

CAPTAIN IDLE
Shall I? [To **PYEBOARD**] Maybe some spirit that haunts the circle.

[**EDMOND** pulls him by the nose.

PYEBOARD
Oh, my nose! Again! Pray conjure then, captain.

EDMOND
Troth, this is ex'lent; I may do any knavery now and never be seen! And now I remember, Sir Godfrey me, my uncle, abus'd me t'other day and told tales of me to my mother. Troth, now I'm invisible, I'll hit him a sound wherret a' th' ear when he comes out a' th' garden. I may be reveng'd on him now finely.

[Enter **SIR GODFREY, WIDOW, FRANK, NICHOLAS** with the chain.

SIR GODFREY
I have my chain again; my chain's found again! Oh, sweet captain! Oh, admirable conjurer!

[**EDMOND** strikes him.

Oh! What mean you by that, nephew?

EDMOND
Nephew? I hope you do not know me, uncle?

WIDOW
Why did you strike your uncle, sir?

EDMOND
Why, captain, am I not invisible?

CAPTAIN IDLE [Aside to **PYEBOARD**]
A good jest, George!—Not now you are not, sir. Why, did you not see me when I did uncharm you?

EDMOND
Not I, by my troth, captain. Then pray you pardon me, uncle; I thought I'd been invisible when I struck you.

SIR GODFREY
So, you would do't! Go, y'are a foolish boy,
And were I not o'ercome with greater joy,
I'd make you taste correction.

EDMOND [Aside]
Correction! Push! No, neither you nor my mother shall think to whip me as you have done.

SIR GODFREY
Captain, my joy is such I know not how to thank you; let me embrace you, hug you. Oh, my sweet chain! Gladness e'en makes me giddy. Rare man! 'Twas just i' th' rosemary-bank, as if one should ha' laid it there. Oh, cunning, cunning!

WIDOW
Well, seeing my fortune tells me I must marry, let me marry a man of wit, a man of parts. Here's a worthy captain, and 'tis a fine title truly, la, to be a captain's wife. A captain's wife! It goes very finely; beside, all the world knows that a worthy captain is a fit companion to any lord: then why not a sweet bedfellow for any lady? I'll have it so.

[Enter **FRAILITY**.

FRAILTY
Oh, mistress, gentlemen, there's the bravest sight coming along this way!

WIDOW
What brave sight?

FRAILTY
Oh, one going to burying, and another going to hanging!

WIDOW
A rueful sight.

PYEBOARD [Aside to **CAPTAIN IDLE**]
'Sfoot, captain, I'll pawn my life the corporal's coffin'd, and old Skirmish the solider going to execution, and 'tis now full about the time of his waking. Hold out a little longer, sleepy potion, and we shall have ex'lent admiration, for I'll take upon me the cure of him.

[Exeunt.

SCENE III - The Street Before the Widow's House

Enter the coffin of **CORPORAL OATH**, the soldier **SKIRMISH** bound and led by **OFFICERS**, the **SHERIFF** there. Enter from the house **SIR GODFREY**, the **WIDOW**, **FRANK**, **CAPTAIN IDLE**, **PYEBOARD**, **EDMOND**, **FRAILITY**, and **NICHOLAS**.

FRAILTY
Oh, here they come, here they come!

PYEBOARD [Aside]
Now must I close secretly with the soldier, prevent his impatience, or else all's discovered.

WIDOW
Oh, lamentable seeing! These were those brothers that fought and bled before our door.

SIR GODFREY
What! They were not, sister!

SKIRMISH [Aside to **PYEBOARD**]
George, look to't; I'll peach at Tyburn else!

PYEBOARD [Aside to **SKIRMISH**]
Mum!—Gentles all, vouchsafe me audience,
And you especially, master sheriff:
Yon man is bound to execution
Because he wounded this that now lies coffin'd?

SHERIFF
True, true; he shall have the law, and I know the law.

PYEBOARD
But under favour, master sheriff, if this man had been cured and safe again, he should have been releas'd then?

SHERIFF
Why make you question of that, sir?

PYEBOARD
Then I release him freely, and will take upon me the death that he should die if within a little season I do not cure him to his proper health again.

SHERIFF
How, sir! Recover a dead man? That were most strange of all.

[**FRANK** comes to **PYEBOARD**.

FRANK
Sweet sir, I love you dearly, and could wish my best part yours. Oh, do not undertake such an impossible venture!

PYEBOARD
Love you me? Then for your sweet sake I'll do't.
Let me entreat the corpse to be set down.

SHERIFF
Bearers, set down the coffin. This were wonderful and worthy Stow's chronicle.

PYEBOARD
I pray bestow the freedom of the air upon our wholesome art. [Aside] Mass, his cheeks begin to receive natural warmth! Nay, good corporal, wake betime, or I shall have a longer sleep than you. 'Sfoot, if he should prove dead indeed now, he were fully reveng'd upon me for making a property on him; yet I had rather run upon the ropes than have a rope like a tetter run upon me. Oh, he stirs! He stirs again!— Look, gentlemen! He recovers! He starts, he rises!

SHERIFF
Oh, oh, defend us! Out, alas!

PYEBOARD
Nay, pray be still; you'll make him more giddy else. He knows nobody yet.

CORPORAL OATH
Zounds, where am I? Cover'd with snow? I marvel!

PYEBOARD [Aside]
Nay, I knew he would swear the first thing he did as soon as ever he came to his life again.

CORPORAL OATH
'Sfoot, hostess, some hot porridge! Oh, oh! Lay on a dozen of faggots in the moon parlour there.

PYEBOARD [To **WIDOW**]
Lady, you must needs take a little pity of him, i'faith, and send him in to your kitchen fire.

WIDOW
Oh, with all my heart, sir. Nicholas and Frailty, help to bear him in.

NICHOLAS
Bear him in, quoth 'a! Pray call out the maids; I shall ne'er have the heart to do't, indeed, la!

FRAILTY
Nor I neither; I cannot abide to handle a ghost, of all men.

CORPORAL OATH
'Sblood, let me see. Where was I drunk last night, heh?

WIDOW
Oh, shall I bid you once again take him away?

FRAILTY
Why, we're as fearful as you, I warrant you. Oh!

WIDOW
Away, villains! Bid the maids make him a caudle presently to settle his brain, or a posset of sack; quickly, quickly.

[Exeunt **FRAILITY** and **NICHOLAS** pushing in **CORPORAL OATH**.

SHERIFF
Sir, whatsoe'er you are, I do more than admire you.

WIDOW
Oh, ay, if you knew all, master sheriff, as you shall do, you would say then that here were two of the rarest men within the walls of Christendom.

SHERIFF
Two of 'em? Oh, wonderful! Officers, I discharge you: set him free; all's in tune.

SIR GODFREY
Ay, and a banquet ready by this time, master sheriff, to which I most cheerfully invite you and your late prisoner there. See you this goodly chain, sir? Mum, no more words: 'twas lost and is found again. Come, my inestimable bullies; we'll talk of your noble acts in sparkling charnico, and instead of a jester, we'll have the ghost i' th' white sheet sit at the upper end a' th' table.

SHERIFF
Ex'lent, merry man, i'faith!

[Exeunt all but **FRANK**.

FRANK
Well, seeing I am enjoin'd to love and marry,
My foolish vow thus I cashier to air,
Which first begot it. Now, love, play thy part;
The scholar reads his lecture in my heart.

[Exit.

SCENE I - The Street Before the Widow's House

Enter in haste **EDMOND** and **FRAILITY**.

EDMOND
This is the marriage-morning for my mother and my sister.

FRAILTY
Oh me, Master Edmond! We shall ha' rare doings.

EDMOND
Nay, go, Frailty, run to the sexton; you know my mother will be married at Saint Antling's. Hie thee; 'tis past five: bid them open the church door; my sister is almost ready.

FRAILTY
What, already, Master Edmond?

EDMOND
Nay, go; hie thee. First run to the sexton, and run to the clerk, and then run to Master Pigman the parson, and then run to the milliner, and then run home again.

FRAILTY
Here's run, run, run—

EDMOND
But hark, Frailty.

FRAILTY
What, more yet?

EDMOND
Has the maids remember'd to strew the way to the church?

FRAILTY
Fagh, an hour ago! I help'd 'em myself.

EDMOND
Away, away, away, away then.

FRAILTY
Away, away, away then.

[Exit **FRAILITY**.

EDMOND
I shall have a simple father-in-law, a brave captain, able to beat all our street: Captain Idle. Now my lady mother will be fitted for a delicate name: my Lady Idle, my Lady Idle, the finest name that can be for a woman. And then the scholar, Master Pyeboard, for my sister Frances, that will be Mistress Frances Pyeboard. Mistress Frances Pyeboard. They'll keep a good table, I warrant you. Now all the knights' noses are put out of joint; they may go to a bone-setter's now.

[Enter **CAPTAIN IDLE** and **PYEBOARD** with **ATTENDANTS**.

Hark, hark! Oh, who come here with two torches before 'em? My sweet captain and my fine scholar! Oh, how bravely they are shot up in one night! They look like fine Britons now, methinks. Here's a gallant change, i'faith! 'Slid, they have hir'd men and all by the clock!

CAPTAIN IDLE
Master Edmond; kind, honest, dainty Master Edmond.

EDMOND
Fogh, sweet captain father-in-law! A rare perfume, i'faith.

PYEBOARD
What, are the brides stirring? May we steal upon 'em, think'st thou, Master Edmond?

EDMOND
Faw, they're e'en upon readiness, I can assure you, for they were at their torch e'en now; by the same token I tumbled down the stairs.

PYEBOARD
Alas, poor Master Edmond.

[Enter **MUSICIANS**.

CAPTAIN IDLE
Oh, the musicians! I prithee, Master Edmond, call 'em in and liquor 'em a little.

EDMOND
That I will, sweet captain father-in-law, and make each of them as drunk as a common fiddler.

[Exeunt **OMNES**.

SCENE II - The Street Before the Widow's House

Enter **SIR JOHN PENNYDUB**, and **MOLL** above lacing her clothes.

SIR JOHN PENNYDUB
Whew! Mistress Moll, Mistress Moll!

MOLL
Who's there?

SIR JOHN PENNYDUB
'Tis I.

MOLL
Who? Sir John Pennydub? Oh, you're an early cock, i'faith! Who would have thought you to be so rare a stirrer?

SIR JOHN PENNYDUB
Prithee, Moll, let me come up.

MOLL
No, by my faith, Sir John; I'll keep you down, for you knights are very dangerous if once you get above.

SIR JOHN PENNYDUB
I'll not stay, i'faith.

MOLL
I'faith you shall stay, for, Sir John, you must note the nature of the climates: your northern wench in her own country may well hold out till she be fifteen, but if she touch the south once and come up to London, here the chimes go presently after twelve.

SIR JOHN PENNYDUB
Oh, th'art a mad wench, Moll; but I prithee make haste, for the priest is gone before.

MOLL
Do you follow him; I'll not be long after.

[Exeunt.

SCENE III - A Room in Sir Oliver Muckhill's House

Enter **SIR OLIVER** Muckhill, **SIR ANDREW** Tipstaff, and old **SKIRMISH** talking.

SIR OLIVER
Oh, monstrous, unheard-of forgery!

SIR ANDREW
Knight, I never heard of such villainy in our own country in my life.

SIR OLIVER

Why, 'tis impossible. Dare you maintain your words?

SKIRMISH

Dare we? Even to their wezen pipes. We know all their plots; they cannot squander with us. They have knavishly abus'd us, made only properties on's, to advance theirselves upon our shoulders, but they shall rue their abuses. This morning they are to be married.

SIR OLIVER

'Tis too true. Yet if the widow be not too much besotted on sleights and forgeries, the revelation of their villainies will make 'em loathsome. And to that end, be it in private to you, I sent late last night to an honourable personage, to whom I am much indebted in kindness, as he is to me; and therefore presume upon the payment of his tongue, and that he will lay out good words for me: and to speak truth, for such needful occasions I only preserve him in bond, and sometimes he may do me more good here in the city by a free word of his mouth than if he had paid one half in hand and took doomsday for t'other.

SIR ANDREW

In troth, sir, without soothing be it spoken, you have publish'd much judgment in these few words.

SIR OLIVER

For you know, what such a man utters will be thought effectual and to weighty purpose, and therefore into his mouth we'll put the approved theme of their forgeries.

SKIRMISH

And I'll maintain it, knight, if ye'll be true.

[Enter a **SERVANT**.

SIR OLIVER

How now, fellow?

SERVANT

May it please you, sir, my lord is newly lighted from his coach.

SIR OLIVER

Is my lord come already? His honour's early.
You see he loves me well. Up before seven!
Trust me, I have found him night-capp'd at eleven.
There's good hope yet; come, I'll relate all to him.

[Exeunt.

SCENE IV - A Street, A Church Appearing

Enter the two bridegrooms, **CAPTAIN IDLE** and scholar **PYEBOARD**; after them, **SIR GODFREY** and **EDMOND, WIDOW** chang'd in apparel, **MISTRESS FRANCIS** led between two K**NIGHTS, SIR JOHN**

PENNYCLUB and **MOLL**, with **NICHOLAS** and other **ATTENDANTS**. There meets them a **NOBLEMAN, SIR OLIVER** Muckhill, and **SIR ANDREW** Tipstaff.

NOBLEMAN
By your leave, lady.

WIDOW
My lord, your honour is most chastely welcome.

NOBLEMAN
Madam, though I came now from court, I come not to flatter you. Upon whom can I justly cast this blot but upon your own forehead, that know not ink from milk? Such is the blind besotting in the state of an unheaded woman that's a widow. For it is the property of all you that are widows, a handful excepted, to hate those that honestly and carefully love you, to the maintenance of credit, state, and posterity, and strongly to dote on those that only love you to undo you. Who regard you least are best regarded; who hate you most are best beloved. And if there be but one man amongst ten thousand millions of men that is accurst, disastrous, and evilly planeted, whom Fortune beats most, whom God hates most, and all societies esteem least, that man is sure to be a husband. Such is the peevish moon that rules your bloods. An impudent fellow best woos you, a flattering lip best wins you, or in a mirth, who talks rougliest is most sweetest; nor can you distinguish truth from forgeries, mists from simplicity: witness those two deceitful monsters that you have entertain'd for bridegrooms.

WIDOW
Deceitful?

PYEBOARD [Aside]
All will out.

CAPTAIN IDLE [Aside to **PYEBOARD**]
'Sfoot, who has blabb'd, George? That foolish Nicholas?

NOBLEMAN
For what they have besotted your easy blood withal were nought but forgeries: the fortune-telling for husbands, the conjuring for the chain Sir Godfrey heard the falsehood of, all nothing but mere knavery, deceit, and cozenage.

WIDOW
Oh, wonderful! Indeed, I wonder'd that my husband, with all his craft, could not keep himself out of purgatory.

SIR GODFREY
And I more wonder'd that my chain should be gone and my tailor had none of it.

MOLL
And I wonder'd most of all that I should be tied from marriage, having such a mind to't. Come, Sir John Pennydub, fair weather on our side: the moon has chang'd since yesternight.

PYEBOARD

The sting of every evil is within me.

NOBLEMAN
And that you may perceive I feign not with you, behold their fellow actor in those forgeries, who, full of spleen and envy at their so sudden advancements, reveal'd all their plot in anger.

[Enter **SKIRMISH**.

PYEBOARD
Base soldier, to reveal us!

WIDOW
Is't possible we should be blinded so and our eyes open?

NOBLEMAN
Widow, will you now believe that false which too soon you believ'd true?

WIDOW
Oh, to my shame I do!

SIR GODFREY
But under favour, my lord, my chain was truly lost and strangely found again.

NOBLEMAN
Resolve him of that, soldier.

SKIRMISH
In few words, knight, then, thou wert the arch-gull of all.

SIR GODFREY
How, sir?

SKIRMISH
Nay, I'll prove it, for the chain was but hid in the rosemary bank all this while, and thou gotst him out of prison to conjure for it, who did it admirably, fustianly, for indeed what need any others when he knew where it was?

SIR GODFREY
Oh, villainy of villainies! But how came my chain there?

SKIRMISH
Where's "Truly-la-indeed-la," he that will not swear, but lie, he that will not steal, but rob: pure Nicholas St. Tantlings?

SIR GODFREY
Oh, villain! One of our society,
Deem'd always holy, pure, religious.
A puritan a thief! When was't ever heard?

Sooner we'll kill a man than steal, thou know'st.
Out, slave! I'll rend my lion from thy back
With mine own hands.

NICHOLAS
Dear master, oh!

NOBLEMAN
Nay, knight, dwell in patience. And now, widow, being so near the church, 'twere great pity, nay, uncharity, to send you home again without a husband. Draw nearer, you of true worship, state, and credit, that should not stand so far off from a widow and suffer forged shapes to come between you. Not that in these I blemish the true title of a captain, or blot the fair margent of a scholar, for I honour worthy and deserving parts in the one, and cherish fruitful virtues in the other. Come, lady, and you, virgin: bestow your eyes and your purest affections upon men of estimation both in court and city that have long wooed you, and both with their hearts and wealth sincerely love you.

[**SIR OLIVER** and **SIR ANDREW** step forward.

SIR GODFREY
Good sister, do. Sweet little Frank, these are men of reputation: you shall be welcome at hour, a great credit for a citizen. Sweet sister.

NOBLEMAN
Come, her silence does consent to't.

WIDOW
I know not with what face—

NOBLEMAN
Pah, pah! Why, with your own face; they desire no other.

WIDOW
Pardon me, worthy sirs: I and my daughter
Have wrong'd your loves.

SIR OLIVER
'Tis easily pardon'd, lady,
If you vouchsafe it now.

WIDOW
With all my soul.

FRANK
And I, with all my heart.

MOLL
And I, Sir John,
With soul, heart, lights and all.

SIR JOHN PENNYDUB
They are all mine, Moll.

NOBLEMAN
Now, lady,
What honest spirit but will applaud your choice
And gladly furnish you with hand and voice?
A happy change, which makes even heaven rejoice.
Come, enter into your joys; you shall not want
For fathers now; I doubt it not, believe me,
But that you shall have hands enough to give ye.

[Exeunt **OMNES**.

Thomas Middleton – A Short Biography

Thomas Middleton was born in London in April 1580 and baptised on 18th April. He was the son of a bricklayer who had raised himself to the status of a gentleman and become the owner of property adjoining the Curtain Theatre in Shoreditch.

Middleton was aged only five when his father died. His mother remarried but this new union unfortunately fell apart and turned into a fifteen year legal conflict centered on the inheritance of Thomas and his younger sister.

Middleton went on to attend Queen's College, Oxford, matriculating in 1598. However he failed to graduate for reasons unknown leaving either in 1600 or 1601. He had by that time written and published three long poems in popular Elizabethan styles. None appears to have been commercially successful although Microcynicon: Six Snarling Satirese was denounced by the Archbishop of Canterbury and publicly burned as part of his attack on verse satire. Although a minor work, the poems show the roots of Middleton's interest in, and later mature work on, sin, hypocrisy, and lust.

In the early years of the 17th century, Middleton made a living writing topical pamphlets, including one, Penniless Parliament of Threadbare Poets, that was reprinted several times as well as becoming the subject of a parliamentary inquiry.

For one so young he was already making quite an impact and had obviously attracted the eye of the authorities in those turbulent times.

Records surviving of the great theatrical entrepreneur of the day, Philip Henslowe, confirm that Middleton was writing for Henslowe's Admiral's Men. His lauded contemporary, a certain William Shakespeare, was writing only for Henslowe whereas Middleton remained a free agent and able to write for whichever theatrical company hired him.

These early years writing plays continued to attract controversy. His friendship and writing partnership with Thomas Dekker brought him into conflict with Ben Jonson and George Chapman in the so-called

War of the Theatres. (This controversy was also called the Poetomachia by Thomas Dekker. The Bishops Ban of 1599 had removed any use of satire from prose and verse publications and so the only outlet was on the stage. For the next 3 years Ben Jonson and George Chapman on one side and John Marston, Thomas Dekker and Thomas Middleton on the other poked fun at their opposition with characters from their plays. The grudge against Jonson continued as late as 1626, when Jonson's play The Staple of News indulges in a slur on Middleton's last play, A Game at Chess).

In 1603, Middleton married. It was also a momentous year in other respects. On the death of Elizabeth I, her cousin James VI of Scotland was now also crowned King James I of England. Another outbreak of the plague now forced the theatres in London to close.

For Middleton the changeover from Elizabethan to Jacobean was the beginning of a long period of success as a writer.

When the theatres re-opened and welcomed back audiences in need of entertainment Middleton was there, writing for several different companies. In particular he specialised in city comedy and revenge tragedy.

During this time he appears also to have written with Shakespeare and he is variously attributed as collaborating on All's Well That Ends Well and Timon of Athens.

Although Middleton had started as a junior partner to Thomas Dekker he was now his fully fledged equal. His finest work with Dekker was undoubtedly The Roaring Girl, a biography of the notorious contemporary thief Mary Frith (Frith began her criminal career as a pickpocket before moving on to highway robbery with a penchant for dressing up as a man. A spell in prison was followed by a long career as a 'fence' from her shop in Fleet St. She lived to the then quite extraordinary age of 74.) The writing is noteworthy not only for its playwriting ambition but in producing a fully formed heroine in Moll Cutpurse. This was only shortly after the role of women in plays had seen fit to have them played, in the main, by men.

In the 1610s, Middleton began another playwriting partnership, this time with the actor William Rowley, producing another slew of plays including the classics Wit at Several Weapons and A Fair Quarrel.

The ever adaptable Middleton seemed at ease working with others or by himself. His solo writing credits include the comic masterpiece, A Chaste Maid in Cheapside, in 1613. Interestingly his solo plays are somewhat less thrusting and bellicose. Certainly there is no comedy among them with the satirical depth of Michaelmas Term and no tragedy as raw, striking and as bloodthirsty as The Revenger's Tragedy.

There may be various reasons for this and among them that he was increasingly involved with civic pageants and therefore was trying to avoid too much controversy especially without the cover of a collaborator. Indeed in 1620, he was officially appointed as chronologer of the City of London, a post he held until his death in 1627, when ironically, it passed to his great rival, and sometime enemy, Ben Jonson.

Middleton's official duties did not interrupt his dramatic writing; the 1620s saw the production of his and Rowley's tragedy, and continual favourite, The Changeling, as well as several other tragicomedies.

However in 1624, he reached a peak of notoriety when his dramatic allegory A Game at Chess was staged by the King's Men. The play used the conceit of a chess game to present and satirise the recent intrigues surrounding the Spanish Match; James I's son, Prince Charles, was being positioned to marry the daughter, Maria Anna of the Spanish King Philip IV of Spain. Though Middleton's approach was strongly patriotic, the Privy Council closed the play, after only nine performances at the Globe theatre, having received a complaint from the Spanish ambassador. The Privy Council then opened a prosecution against both authors and actors. Although Middleton in his defence showed that the play had been passed by the Master of the Revels, Sir Henry Herbert, any further performance was forbidden and the author and actors fined.

What happened next is a mystery. It is the last play recorded as having being written by Middleton. His playwriting career appears to have stopped dead. It follows that some sort of further punishment probably occurred and for a writer can there be any greater punishment than not being allowed to write or be heard?

Middleton's work is diverse even by the standards of his age. His career Middleton covers many many genres including tragedy, history and city comedy. As we have noted he did not have the kind of official relationship with a particular company that Shakespeare or Fletcher had that might have supported him in a lean creative period. Instead he appears to have written on a freelance basis for any number of companies. His output ranges from the "snarling" satire of Michaelmas Term, performed by the Children of Paul's, to the bleak intrigues of The Revenger's Tragedy, performed by the King's Men. Interestingly earlier editions of The Revenger's Tragedy attributed the play solely to Cyril Tourneur but recent studies have shredded that view so that Middleton's authorship is not now seriously contested

Indeed modern techniques in analysing writing styles are now leaning towards giving Middleton credit for his adaptation and revision of Shakespeare's Macbeth and Measure for Measure. Along with the more established evidence of collaboration on All's Well That Ends Well and Timon of Athens it appears that Middleton has moved some way forward to the front rank of playwrights and an association, in some form, but its greatest exponent.

His early work was informed by the blossoming, in the late Elizabethan period, of satire, while his maturity was influenced by the ascendancy of Fletcherian tragicomedy. Middleton's later work, in which his satirical fury is tempered and broadened, includes three of his acknowledged masterpieces. A Chaste Maid in Cheapside, produced by the Lady Elizabeth's Men, which skillfully combines London life with an expansive view of the power of love to effect reconciliation even though London seems populated entirely by sinners, in which no social rank goes unsatirised. The Changeling, a later tragedy, returns Middleton to an Italianate setting like that of The Revenger's Tragedy, except that here the central characters are more fully drawn and more compelling as individuals. Similar development can be seen in Women Beware Women.

Middleton's plays are marked by their cynicism, though often very funny, about the human race. His characters are complex. True heroes are a rarity: almost all of his characters are selfish, greedy, and self-absorbed.

When Middleton does portray good people, the characters are often presented as flawless and perfect and given small, undemanding roles. A theological pamphlet attributed to Middleton gives sustenance to the notion that Middleton was a strong believer in Calvinism.

Thomas Middleton died at his home at Newington Butts in Southwark in the summer of 1627, and was buried on July 4th, in St Mary's churchyard which today survives as a public park in Elephant and Castle.

Middleton stands with John Fletcher and Ben Jonson as the most successful and prolific of playwrights from the Jacobean period. Very few Renaissance dramatists would achieve equal success in both comedy and tragedy but Middleton was one. He also wrote many masques and pageants and remains, to this day, one of the most notable of Jacobean dramatists.

Middleton's work has long been praised by many literary critics, among the most fervent were Algernon Charles Swinburne and T. S. Eliot. The latter thought Middleton was second only to Shakespeare.

Among their contemporaries was a very crowded field of talent including: Ben Jonson (1572-1637), Christopher Marlowe (1564-1593), Francis Beaumont (1585-1616), Henry Chettle (1564-1606), John Fletcher (1579–1625), John Ford (1586–1639), John Day (1574-1640), John Marston (1576-1634), John Webster (1580-1634), Nathan Field (1587-1620), Philip Massinger (1584-1640), Richard Burbage (1567-1619), Robert Greene (1558-1592), Thomas Dekker (1575-1625), Thomas Kyd (1558-1594), William Haughton (died 1605), William Rowley (1585-1626).

It's a daunting list and confirms that to top that made you a very special talent indeed.

Thomas Middleton – A Concise Bibliography

It has long been recognised that the modern concept of authorship was rather more elastic in centuries past. Writers were not only for hire, and their work therefore a commodity, but their plays ran much shorter lengths; two weeks being a common term of performance. To that themes and scenes were liberally excised from one play and used in another. Revisions to past plays that were being restaged would be undertaken and entirely credited to other writers. Many works and plays were unpublished and have not survived and some only from memory by actors etc. Whilst many of these playwrights are only now feted for their talents, some undoubtedly were at the time, but it is difficult to, in every case, to establish exact provenance. With modern scholarly and literary techniques author attributions have sometimes changed or been re-balanced. For those where this may be the case we have placed the *Play's Title and other information* in italics

Plays
Blurt, Master Constable or The Spaniard's Night Walk (with Thomas Dekker (1602)
The Phoenix (1603–4)
The Honest Whore, Part 1, a city comedy (1604), (with Thomas Dekker)
Michaelmas Term, a city comedy, (1604)
All's Well That Ends Well (1604-5); believed by some to be co-written by Middleton based on stylometric analysis.
A Trick to Catch the Old One, a city comedy (1605)
A Mad World, My Masters, a city comedy (1605)
A Yorkshire Tragedy, a one-act tragedy (1605); attributed to Shakespeare on its title page, but stylistic analysis favours Middleton.

Timon of Athens a tragedy (1605–6); stylistic analysis indicates that Middleton may have written this play in collaboration with William Shakespeare.

The Puritan (1606)

The Revenger's Tragedy (1606). Earlier editions often mistakenly attribute authorship to Cyril Tourneur.

Your Five Gallants, a city comedy (1607)

The Family of Love (1607) some attribute this to Middleton others include Dekker and Lording Barry.

The Bloody Banquet (1608–9); co-written with Thomas Dekker.

The Roaring Girl, a city comedy depicting the exploits of Mary Frith (1611); with Thomas Dekker.

No Wit, No Help Like a Woman's, a tragic-comedy (1611)

The Second Maiden's Tragedy, a tragedy (1611); an anonymous manuscript; stylistic analysis indicates Middleton's authorship (though one scholar also attributed it to Shakespeare.

A Chaste Maid in Cheapside, a city comedy (1613)

Wit at Several Weapons, a city comedy (1613); printed as part of the Beaumont and Fletcher Folio, but stylistic analysis indicates comprehensive revision by Middleton & Rowley.

More Dissemblers Besides Women, a tragicomedy (1614)

The Widow (1615–16)

The Witch, a tragicomedy (1616)

A Fair Quarrel, a tragicomedy (1616). Co-written with William Rowley.

The Old Law, a tragicomedy (1618–19). written with William Rowley and perhaps a third collaborator.

Hengist, King of Kent, or The Mayor of Quinborough, a tragedy (1620)

Women Beware Women, a tragedy (1621)

Measure for Measure (1603-4); some scholars argue that the First Folio text was partly revised by Middleton in 1621.

Anything for a Quiet Life, a city comedy (1621). Co-written with John Webster.

The Changeling, a tragedy (1622). Co-written with William Rowley.

The Nice Valour (1622). Printed as part of the Beaumont and Fletcher Folio, but stylistic analysis indicates comprehensive revision by Middleton.

The Spanish Gypsy, a tragicomedy (1623). Believed to be a play by Middleton & Rowley and later revised by Thomas Dekker and John Ford.

A Game at Chess, a political satire (1624). Satirized the negotiations over the proposed marriage of Prince Charles, son of James I of England, with the Spanish princess. Closed after nine performances.

Masques & Entertainments

The Whole Royal and Magnificent Entertainment Given to King James Through the City of London (1603–4). Co-written with Thomas Dekker, Stephen Harrison & Ben Jonson.

The Manner of his Lordship's Entertainment

The Triumphs of Truth

Civitas Amor

The Triumphs of Honour and Industry (1617)

The Masque of Heroes, or, The Inner Temple Masque (1619)

The Triumphs of Love and Antiquity (1619)

The World Tossed at Tennis (1620). Co-written with William Rowley.

Honourable Entertainments (1620–1)

An Invention (1622)

The Sun in Aries (1621)

The Triumphs of Honour and Virtue (1622)

The Triumphs of Integrity with The Triumphs of the Golden Fleece (1623)

The Triumphs of Health and Prosperity (1626)

Poetry
The Wisdom of Solomon Paraphrased (1597)
Microcynicon: Six Snarling Satires (1599)
The Ghost of Lucrece (1600)
Burbage epitaph (1619)
Bolles epitaph (1621)
Duchess of Malfi (commendatory poem) (1623)
St James (1623)
To the King (1624)

Prose
The Penniless Parliament of Threadbare Poets (1601)
News from Gravesend. Co-written with Thomas Dekker (1603)
The Nightingale and the Ant aka Father Hubbard's Tales (1604)
The Meeting of Gallants at an Ordinary (1604). Co-written with Thomas Dekker.
Plato's Cap Cast at the Year 1604 (1604)
The Black Book (1604)
Sir Robert Sherley his Entertainment in Cracovia (1609) (translation).
The Two Gates of Salvation (1609), or The Marriage of the Old and New Testament.
The Owl's Almanac (1618)
The Peacemaker (1618)